MW01029144

Global
3

More Songs for Worship
and
Witness

S T Kimbrough, Jr.
Editor

Carlton R. Young
Musical Editor

Jorge Lockward
Barbara Day Miller
Assistant Editors

The General Board of Global Ministries
The United Methodist Church
GBGMusik

Published by the General Board of Global Ministries
GBGMusik,
475 Riverside Drive,
New York, NY 10115

The Global Praise products may be ordered from:

COKESBURY
201 – 8th Avenue, South
Nashville, TN 37202
Tel. 1-800-672-1789

SERVICE CENTER
7820 Reading Road
Cincinnati, OH 45222-1800
Tel. 1-800-505-9857

GBGMusik
475 Riverside Drive, Room 350
New York, NY 10115
Tel. 1-212-870-3633

ISBN 1-890569-87-9

Manufactured in the United States of America

Acknowledgments

Once again gratitude is expressed to the members of the Global Praise Working Group of the General Board of Global Ministries whose assistance in developing the repertory of this songbook has been invaluable: Abraham Arpellet, Tomas Boström, Melva Costen, Ludmila Pavlovna Garbuzova, Hartmut Handt, Per Harling, Marilyn Hofstra, Ivor H. Jones, Mary K. Jackson, S T Kimbrough, Jr., Jorge Lockward, I-to Loh, Lim Swee Hong, Patrick Matsikenyiri, Simei Monteiro, George Mulrain, David Plüss, Piret Pormeister-Rips, Joyce Sohl, Pablo Sosa, Carlton R. Young. Sincere appreciation is expressed also to Irina Miagkova, David Wu, and many others for their assistance with languages.

Very special words of thanks are expressed to the team of editors who worked untiringly with the editor on this songbook: especially to Carlton R. Young, the indefatible music editor, and to assistant editors Jorge Lockward and Barbara Day Miller for their excellent work.

To all those who contributed in any way to the formation and completion of this volume deepest gratitude is expressed.

GLOBAL PRAISE 3:
MORE SONGS FOR WORSHIP AND WITNESS

SONGS FOR WORSHIP

SONGS OF WITNESS

God's Witness

The Christian's Witness

HOPE AND JOY

Copyright Acknowledgments

Index of Countries

Index of Scriptural References

Index of Authors, Composers, Translators, and Others

Index of First Lines and Common Titles

Introduction

The songbook *Global Praise 3: More Songs for Worship and Witness* is the third major collection of songs from around the world published by GBGMusik of the General Board of Global Ministries (GBGM) of The United Methodist Church. As previously, many of the contributors are from the Global Praise Working Group of authors and composers which meets annually and whose members continue to provide guidance and formation to the *Global Praise Program* of GBGM.

The *Global Praise Program* was begun in 1993 by GBGM as a means of gathering, receiving, and sharing the songs of the people called Methodists and other Christians around the world. As the Christian faith has spread throughout the world, the constancy of the enduring gospel message has become expressed in songs of incredible diversity. Hence, as Christians relate to one another and to others, to build community, it is essential to share their songs. This is the reason for the *Global Praise Program*, which brings together authors and composers from the global Methodist connection and the ecumenical community to share their creative skills in witness. It seeks to discover the music, texts, and rhythms, which can be shared viably and effectively to strengthen and affirm one another in the faith pilgrimage, and to proclaim the gospel of Jesus Christ to all. It seeks to enable and facilitate indigenous song among people wherever they are to enrich life, worship, and witness.

Global Praise 3 has essentially the same structure as *Global Praise 2*, with a few internal thematic changes. The first half of the book is entitled *Songs for Worship* and includes selections for many aspects of divine worship, including service music such as *agnus dei, kyrie eleison, alleluia, sanctus, memorial acclamation, Gloria,* as well as a Cambodian setting of "The Lord's Prayer." There are hymns and songs for Holy Communion and baptism, as well as Psalm settings, morning and evening hymns, and prayers and benedictions.

The second half of the book is entitled *Songs of Witness*. The first section stresses God's witness in creation and among humankind: the Trinity, Advent, Christmas, and Christ's passion. The second section emphasizes the Christian's witness under such themes as service and discipleship, the church, unity, mission, peace, justice, love, and hope. The pages listing the contents outline the book in detail, providing all major sections, subheadings, and page numbers.

There are songs from Africa, Asia, the Caribbean, Europe, North and South America, and the Pacific islands. Therefore, fulfill with joy the admonition of the psalmist: "Sing to the Lord a new song!" Affirm one another in the music, words, and rhythms of a worldwide community of faith!

S T Kimbrough, Jr.,
Editor

Haleluya! Pujilah Tuhan

Hallelujah! Praise the Lord

1

words and music, Godlief Soumokil, Indonesia
English trans, Ester Pudjo Widiasih

♩ = 70

Bahasa Indonesia: Ha - le - lu - ya!   Ha - le - lu - ya!
English: Hal - le - lu - jah!   Hal - le - lu - jah!

Pu - ji - lah Tu - han - mu s'la - ma - nya ha - le - lu - ya!____
Praise the Lord ev - er - more praise the Lord, hal - le - lu - jah!____

_ Nya - nyi dan so - rak - lah, a - gung - kan
_ Shout with joy, lift your voice, glo - ri - fy God's

na - ma - Nya. Pu - ji - lah Tu - han - mu
ho - ly name. Praise the Lord ev - er - more,

s'la - ma - nya, Ha - le - lu - ya.
praise the Lord, Hal - le - lu - jah!

Small drum:

Large drum:

2

Yo sé que estás aquí
I know that you are here

author unknown, Honduras
Eng. trans., S T Kimbrough, Jr.

harm., Jorge Lockward

Spanish: Yo sé que es-tás a-quí, mi Se-ñor, yo sé que es-tás a-quí. Yo sé que es-tás a-quí, mi Se-ñor, yo sé que es-tás a-quí. Y mi al-ma te a-la-ba y mi al-ma te a-la-ba, y mi al-ma te a-

English: I know that you are here, my God, I know that you are here. I know that you are here, my God, I know that you are here. And my soul gives you praise, O how my soul gives you praise, O how my soul gives you

Eng. trans. and harm. © 2004 General Board of Global Ministries, GBGMusik, 475 Riverside Dr., New York, NY 10115. All rights reserved.

la - ba por - que sé que es - tás a quí. Y mi al - ma te a-
praise, be - cause I know that you are here. And my soul gives you

la - ba por - que sé que es - tás a - quí.
praise, be - cause I know that you are here.

Mi pela i bung

God of all the world

3

trad. melody, Papua New Guinea
transcr., I-to Loh

Eng. trans., Fred Kaan, UK

Tok Pisin: Mi pe - la i bung pa - pa God long on - rim yu na long
God of all the world, we have come to give you thanks and be-

ten - kim yu tru. tru. Long dis - pe la
come more like you. you. In wor - ship we

lo tu ol pi - pel i bung wan - taim yu.
long to be one with each oth - er and you.

Drum

simile

4 Lo, God is here

Gerhard Tersteegen, Germany
Eng. trans., John Wesley, alt.*

Tomas Boström, Sweden
adapt. and arr., Carlton R. Young

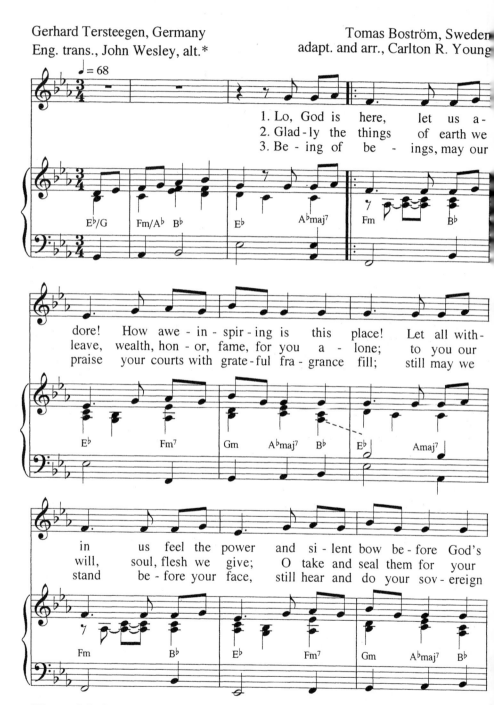

1. Lo, God is here, let us a-dore! How awe-in-spir-ing is this place! Let all with-in us feel the power and si-lent bow be-fore God's in will,
2. Glad-ly the things of earth we leave, wealth, hon-or, fame, for you a-lone; to you our soul, flesh we give; O take and seal them for your
3. Be-ing of be-ings, may our praise your courts with grate-ful fra-grance fill; still may we stand be-fore your face, still hear and do your sov-ereign

*Trans. of Gerhard Tersteegen's "Gott ist gegenwärtig" (1729), *Hymns and Sacred Poems* (1739), orig. stanzas 1,3,4.

2. Glad-ly the
3. Be - ing of

rit.

5   How shall we find you

Shirley Erena Murray, New Zealand

I-to Loh, Taiwan

1. How shall we find you, God who is Ho - ly,
2. How shall we know you, God who is Wis - dom,
3. How shall we trust you, God in the scrip - tures,
4. How shall we see you if not in peo - ple
5. How shall we love you if not as hu - man,

cap - tured by gen - der, col - or and code?
ar - gued by schol - ars, proofed on a page:
fil - tered through lens - es, bi - ased and blurred:
knit to your na - ture, fo - cused in sight__
lov - ing us whol - ly, fleshed on our frame,

How shall we wor - ship, God of the Pres - ence,
how to i - mag - ine, God of cre - a - tion,
how to re - vere you, God of tra - di - tion,
an - gels and art - ists, teach - ers and heal - ers,
known to our hun - ger, known in the meet - ing

ac - tion and es - sence, mean-ing and mode?
world be - yond think - ing, here on our stage?
cased in our church - es, Word bound to word?
heart - and - soul peo - ple, chil - dren of light.
spir - it to Spir - it, nam - ing our name.

6

Ven, te invito
Come and join our song

Spain, author unknown
English trans., Jorge Lockward

♩ = 80

Spanish: Ven, te in-vi-to a can-tar al Se-ñor,
English: Come and join our song of praise to the Lord.

ven, te in-vi-to a de-lei-tar-te en él;
Come! Re-joice, de-light in God's sweet em-brace!

ven, te in-vi-to a can-tar al Se-ñor con
Come and join our song of praise to the Lord with

to-da tu voz, con to-do tu a-mor.
all of your heart, with all of your voice.

Sue-nen vio-li-nes, to-quen trom-pe-tas;
Sound flutes and or-gans, bring strings and trum-pets,

al-zad las vo-ces, ¡A-la-bad a Dios!
lift up your voic-es; praise God's ho-ly name!

Hom-bres y mu-je-res, ni-ños y an-cia-nos,
All the men and wo-men, chil-dren and the el-ders,

sa - nos y en - fer - mos   ¡A - la - bad a Dios! ¡Hey!
join in song to - geth - er,   praise God's ho - ly name! Hey!

Jesus A, Nahetotaetanome   7
Jesus Lord, how joyful

Cheyenne text, John Heap of Birds
Eng. trans., David Graber and others   Plains Indian melody, North America

Je - sus A,   Na - he - to - tae - ta - no - me
Je - sus Lord, how joy - ful you   have   made   us

tseh - ma - no' - ee' - to - va - tse - me - no - to,
to   come   to - geth - ther here   with   you   now!

tse - 'o - noo - me - me - no - to.
In   your   mer - cy   you   have   called   us.

"Na - nee - hoo - ve   me - o - 'o,"
You   say,   "I   am   the   way."

tsex - he - še - me - no - to.   Neh - pa - ve -
We   hear   you   call   us.   We   ask   you,

a - me - otše - se - me - no   ne - me - o - ne - va!
"Come, lead   us   day   by   day."   We fol - low your   way.

© 1982 Mennonite Indian Leaders' Council. Used by permission.

8 Hvala Tebi moj nebeski
Thanks and praise to you, O God

Petar Žunić, Croatia
Eng. para., S T Kimbrough, Jr.

Zdenko Runjić, Croatia

Croatian: 1. Hva - la Te - bi moj ne - be - ski O - če!
2. Zna - o si Ti što ce Te - be ko - štat!

English: 1. Thanks and praise to you, O God in heav - en,
2. You knew what the price would be for giv - ing

Hva - lu Te - bi di - je - te dati ho - če!
Ži - vot svoj za gre - šni - ke po - ložit!

from your child on earth is hum - bly giv - en!
sin - ners par - doned life a - mong the liv - ing.

Ti si da - o svo - je naj - mi - li - je!
Al' Tvoja ljubav ne - o - gra - ni - če - na!

You have shown me love be - yond all mea - sure,
Love e - ter - nal is your pro - clam - a - tion

Da me spa - siš pa - kla, pro - va - li - je!
Ži - vot no - vi po - bje - dom na vje - šta!

sav - ing me from sin, as was your plea - sure.
of the new life found through your sal - va - tion.

Tvo - ja lju - bav ja - ča je od gro - ba!
U Te - bi je sve po - sta - lo no - vo!

Death you've con - quered with your love trans - cend - ing:
You have made all things a new cre - a - tion,

U svom Si - na Ti je oči - to - va!
Tvo - ja Cr - kva pri - pra - vna za ne - bo!

Christ, your Son, re - veals the life un - end - ing.
made the church on earth a heav'n - ly sta - tion.

Refrain

Sla - va Te - bi O - če, Stvori - te - lju, Bo - že!
Sla - va Te - bi Kri ste, ži - vot svoj Ti da - de!

Praise to God Cre - a - tor; praise the one tri - une God,
Praise to God, Christ Je - sus, for the life you've giv - en:

1.

I - zgu blje - no tra - žis da mu se - smi - lu - ješ!
Da u Du - hu Tvo - me

for you seek the lost ones, to em - brace them with love.
in your liv - ing Spi - rit

2.

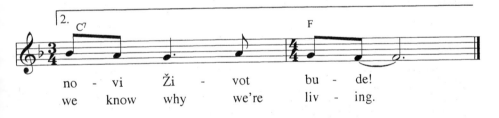

no - vi Ži - vot bu - de!
we know why we're liv - ing.

9 Shiwana yambuka
Rise up, all you nations

Toivo Ndevaetela, alt., Namibia

trad. melody, Namibia

10 Everyone's rejoicing

adapt., Tom Colvin, from a hymn by
H. M. Tweya

M'MWIMBIRE CHIUTA
trad. Tumbuka tune, Malawi
adapt., Tom Colvin

♩ = 92

1. Ev - ery - one's re - joic - ing, ev - ery - one is
2. Chi - u - ta our mak - er is the world's cre -
3. Chi - u - ta sent Ye - su, chains and fet - ters
4. Dear - ly Ye - su loves us, sets his heart up -
5. Peace with jus - tice mak - ing is the kind of
6. Come, Chi - u - ta's peo - ple, come, we are to -

sing - ing, prais - es to Chi - u - ta,*
a - tor. For Chi - u - ta drums beat
break - ing, bless - ed free - dom giv - ing,
on us, leads us to Chi - u - ta,
lov - ing called for by Chi - u - ta,
geth - er, one in Ye - su sing - ing

Refrain

al - le - lu - ya. A - men, al - le - lu - ya, a - men, al - le -
al - le - lu - ya.
al - le - lu - ya.
al - le - lu - ya.
al - le - lu - ya.
al - le - lu - ya.

lu - ya, a - men, al - le - lu - ya, al - le - lu - ya.

*Chiuta (chee-oó-ta) is one name for God in Malawi. The hymn should be sung with a simple and strong drum accompaniment.

Te alabaré, Señor

I give you thanks, O God

11

Ps. 9:1-2
Eng. trans., U. Mantovani and T. MacArthur

author unknown, Ecuador
arr., Jorge Lockward

Spanish: Te a - la - ba - ré, Se - ñor, con to - do mi co - ra-
English: I give you thanks, O God, with all my heart. I will

zón, con to - do mi co - ra - zón te a -
sing with all my heart. I will sing and

la - ba - ré, Se - ñor. Can - ta - ré
give you thanks, O God. I will sing

to - das tus ma - ra - vi - llas, to - das tus ma - ra -
all your mar - vel - ous won - ders, all your mar - vel - ous

12 Rendons gloire à Dieu
To our God we bring adoration

words and music, Alain Burnand, Switzerland

French:
1. Ren - dons gloire à Dieu no - tre Pè - re, ___ bé - nis - sons no - tre Ré - demp - teur___ et que l'Es - prit Saint nous li - bé - re de la tris - tesse et de la peur.

2. Que la joie de Dieu nous ha - bi - te, ___ que la paix de no - tre Sei - gneur___ i - ci - bas ja - mais ne nous quit - te, mais qu'elle é - clai - re no - tre cœur.

3. Al - le - lu, al - le - lu - ia. ___ Al - le - lu, al - le - lu - ia. ___ Al - le - lu, al - le - lu - ia. Al - le - lu - ia, al - le - lu - ia.

To our God we bring adoration 13
Rendons gloire à Dieu

words and music, Alain Burnand, Switzerland
Eng. trans., S T Kimbrough, Jr.

1. To our God we bring ad - o - ra - tion,____
2. God on high fills us with e - la - tion,____
3. Al - le - lu, al - le - lu - ia.____

____ our Re - deem - er we re - vere,____
____ who the peace of Christ im - parts.____
____ Al - le - lu, al - le - lu - ia.____

____ and the Spir - it of lib - er - a - tion,
____ Here be - low there's no sep - a - ra - tion,
____ Al - le - lu, al - le - lu - ia.

who frees from sor - row and from fear.
for our God dwells in faith - ful hearts.
Al - le - lu - ia, al - le - lu - ia.

14   How great your name

words and music, Paschal Jordan, O.S.B., Guyana
Ps. 8:1, and 150

arr., P. E. P.

1. O praise the Lord with - in the As - sem - bly!
2. O praise the Lord with sound of the trum - pet!
3. O praise the Lord with drum and with cym - bal!

Praise the Lord through - out all the world! O praise the Lord be - cause
Praise the Lord with harp and gui - tar! O praise the Lord with dance
Praise the Lord with all that you are! All liv - ing things, come, praise

D. S. al Fine

___ of his great - ness! Al - le - lu! Al - le - lu - ia! How
___ and per - cus - sion! Al - le - lu! Al - le - lu - ia! How
___ your Cre - a - tor! Al - le - lu! Al - le - lu - ia! How

15

Ded-deen dedd
Lord of lords

author and composer unknown, Mongolia
Eng. para., S T Kimbrough, Jr.

1. Ded - deen dedd haad - een haan bol - son Ed - zen Ye - sus-
2. Mon - kheeg monkh hair - een deed bol - son Ed - zen Ye - sus-

1. Lord of lords, King of kings and Lord of lords. We lift
2. Je - sus lives ev - er - more in faith-ful hearts, and his

een al - dreeg on - dort magt - ia. Mag-tan dool - ia Edz-nee nair eeg
een nair - eeg op - gon magt - ia.

high the name: Je - sus our Lord. We will lift up God's ho -ly name
love is great, great-er than all!

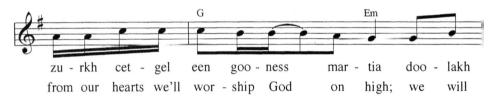

zu - rkh cet - gel een goo - ness mar - tia doo - lakh
from our hearts we'll wor - ship God on high; we will

Doo - nee - khaa ded - deeg Ed - zend or - go - eoo. eoo.
sing, "Hal - le - lu - jah!" prais - ing God on high. high.

Hallelujah, amen

words and music, Nolan Williams, Jr., USA

17 Du allein bist Gott
You alone are God

Martin Rüd, Switzerland   David Plüss, Switzerland

Du al - lein bist Gott und Herr

German: Du al - lein bist Gott und Herr

Du al - lein bist Gott und Herr

Du al - lein bist Gott und Herr

in die - ser Welt und Zeit. Wir die - nen
trotz al - ler Angst und Not. Wir fol - gen
wird uns auch manch - mal bang. Wir rüh - men
in uns - rer klei - nen Welt. Wir dan - ken

dir,   zu dei - ner Ehr'   voll
dir,   und dei - ner Lehr' und
dich,   le - bend' - ger Herr mit
dir,   du Hei - li - ger, dass

Freud   und   Dank - bar - keit.
hal - ten   dein   Ge - bot.
froh - hem   Lob - ge - sang.
dei - ne   Treu   uns hält.

You alone are God
Du allein bist Gott

18

Martin Rüd, Switzerland
Eng. trans., S T Kimbrough, Jr.

David Plüss, Switzerland

You a - lone are God who rules
You a - lone are God who rules
You a - lone are God who rules
You a - lone are God who rules

through - out the world and time; we wor - ship
in spite of fear and need. We fol - low
ev'n when our days are long. We praise you,
in this small world of ours. Most Ho - ly

you, we hon - or you, with
you and what you teach in
God, O liv - ing God, with
One, re - ceive our thanks, for

joy and thanks sub - lime.
thought, and word, and deed.
this, our joy - ful song.
we trust in your powers.

19 Cordero de Dios
O Lamb of God

Toño Robira, Panama
from *La Santa Misa Criolla Panameña*

liturgical text

Cor - de - ro de Dios, Cor - de - ro de
O Lamb of God, who takes a -

Dios, tú que qui - tas el pe - ca - do del
way the sin of the world, have

mun - do, ten pie - dad
mer - cy, have mer -

de no - so - tros. Cor -
- cy, Lord, on us. O

dá - nos la paz,   dá - nos la paz.
grant us your peace,   grant us your peace.

Aliluia

20

trad. chant, Romania

A - li - lu - i - a,   a - li - lu - i -
a,   a - li - lu - i - a.

Halle, hallelujah

21

as taught by Metropolitan Mar Gregorios Yohanna Ibrahim, Syria

Hal - le, hal - le - lu - jah.   Hal - le, hal - le - lu - jah.

Hal - le - lu - jah, hal - le - lu - jah,   hal - le - lu - jah.

Hal - le - lu - jah, hal - le - lu - jah,   hal - le - lu - jah.

22 Halleluya

words and music, Abraham Maraire, Zimbabwe

♩ = 126

Refrain

SA. Hal - le - lu - ya, hal - le - lu - ya,

T. Hal - le - lu - ya, hal - le - lu,

B. Hal - le - lu - ya, hal - le - lu - ya,

Fine

hal - le - lu - ya, hal - le - lu - ya!

hal - le - lu - ya, hal - le - lu - ya!

hal - le - lu - ya, hal - le - lu - ya!

Leader

Shona: 1. Nga - ri - ku - dzwe zu - va i - ro a - no mu - ka - a.
2. Kri - si - to zwi - ku - ru kwa - ti - ri wa - pi - wa.

English: 1. Lift up your voice, sing for joy, for Je - sus is ri - sen.
2. Christ is our friend and shows us God's love for all peo - ple.

All

Hal - le - lu - ya, hal - le - lu - ya!

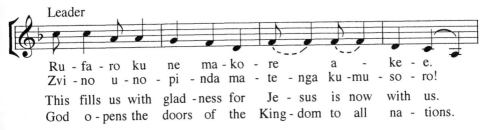

Leader

Ru - fa - ro ku ne ma - ko - re   a - ke - e.
Zvi - no u - no - pi - nda ma - te - nga ku -mu - so - ro!
This fills us with glad -ness for Je - sus is now with us.
God o - pens the doors of the King - dom to all na - tions.

All   *D C. al Fine*

Hal - le - lu - ya,   hal - le - lu - ya.

Alleluia! Praise the Lord   **23**

words and music, Elison Suri, Solomon Islands

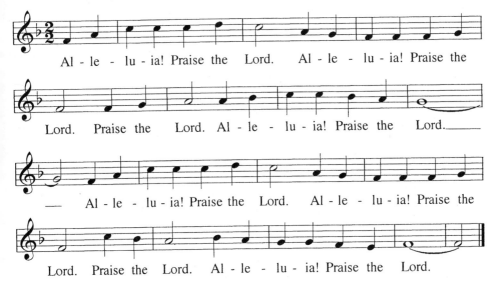

Al - le - lu - ia! Praise the Lord. Al - le - lu - ia! Praise the

Lord. Praise the Lord. Al - le - lu - ia! Praise the Lord.____

___ Al - le - lu - ia! Praise the Lord. Al - le - lu - ia! Praise the

Lord. Praise the Lord. Al - le - lu - ia! Praise the Lord.

24 Alleluia, Amen
Canon

Colville N. Young, Belize

Al - le - lu - ia, a - men, al - le - lu - ia,

Al - le - lu - ia, a - men, al - le - lu - ia.

Lift up your voice. Let

all re - joice in the schools,

a - men, on the farms, a - men,

in the vil - lag - es, a - men,

ev - ery - where in the land, a - men.

Al - le - lu - ia.

Aleluya Y'in Oluwa
Alleluia, praise the Lord

25

author unknown, Nigeria

as taught by Emmanuel Badejo, Nigeria

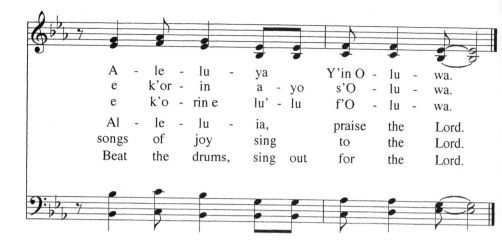

A - le - lu - ya   Y'in O - lu - wa.
e   k'or - in   a - yo   s'O - lu - wa.
e   k'o - rin e   lu' - lu   f'O - lu - wa.

Al - le - lu - ia,   praise the Lord.
songs of joy sing   to the Lord.
Beat the drums, sing out for the Lord.

26 Halleluja

Orthodox chant
Kiev, Ukraine

Hal - le - lu - ja, hal - le - lu - ja,

hal - le - lu - ja.

Alleluia Yehovah

Alleluia Jehovah

27

Michée Ahouandjino, Togo

Voices I and III sing the same text throughout

French words by N. Omolo © 1987 All Africa Conference of Churches. Source: *L'Afrique Chante.* Transcr. © 1986 World Council of Churches. Used by permission.

28 Gloria

words and music, Ulises Torres, Chile

harm., Jorge Lockward

Spanish: ¡Glo - ria! ¡glo - ria!

¡glo - ria!   al   Dios Crea - dor.

Last time to Coda ⊕

ble;
rias.

y la tie-rra es tes - ti - mo - nio de su a-
Que ha - ya paz en la tie - rra, con jus-

mor in - a - go - ta - ble;
ti - cia y sin mi - se - rias.

dor.

Gloria

29

words and music, Ulises Torres, Chile
Eng. trans., S T Kimbrough, Jr.

harm., Jorge Lockward

Refrain

¡Glo - ria! ¡glo - ria!

¡glo - ria!   Sing   we   to   God.

Last time to Coda 𝄌

Glo - ry!, Glo - ry! Glo - ry   to   the   God   of

after stz. 1: Glo - ry to our Lord Je - sus,   Re - deem - er

after stz. 2: Glo - ry to God the Spir - it,   our Com - fort -

love.

God.

er.

1. The heav'ns are tell-ing God's

2. Glo - ry to God of the

glo - ry,   of the glo - ry that can - not be told.   The

An - des,   of the prai - ries, and all of the seas.

earth,   O Lord,   bears wit - ness   to your love that is un - end-

Let there be peace on the   earth,   filled with jus - tice and no mis'-

ing.
ry.

The earth, O Lord bears wit - ness to your
Let there be peace on the earth, filled with

love that is un - end - ing.
jus - tice and no mis' - ry.

D.C. al Coda

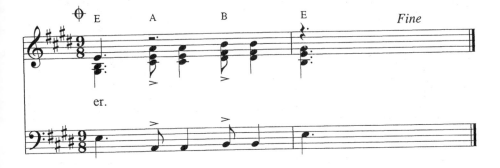

er.

Fine

30

Eer aan God
Glory to our God

words and music, Marcus Veenstra, Netherlands
from the *Jongerenliturgie*
Eng. trans., S T Kimbrough, Jr.

harm., Horacio Vivares

Eer aan God, eer aan God,
Glo - ry to our God,

eer aan God in de he - e - mel.
to our God in the high - est.

Vre - de voor - jou, vre - de voor mij,
Peace be with you, peace be with me,

vre - - de voor
peace be with

ons op de a - ar - de!
all through - out the earth.

Karthave, kirubaiyayirum 31
Gracious Lord, have mercy

Tamil translit., and Eng. trans.,
M. Thomas Thangaraj

M. S. Jesudason, India
transcr., M. Thomas Thangaraj, India

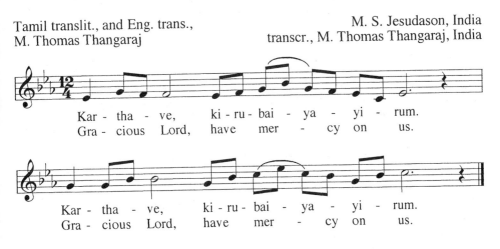

Kar - tha - ve, ki - ru - bai - ya - yi - rum.
Gra - cious Lord, have mer - cy on us.

Kar - tha - ve, ki - ru - bai - ya - yi - rum.
Gra - cious Lord, have mer - cy on us.

When sung as a prayer, line one is sung after the first prayer, line two is sung after the second prayer, and so forth. Line one is sung following the last prayer.

Eng. trans, translit., and transcr. © 2004 General Board of Global Ministries, GBGMusik, 475 Riverside Dr., New York, NY 10115. All rights reserved.

32

Ya, Tuhanku
O Lord, our God

liturgical text

Calvin Chelliah, Malaysia

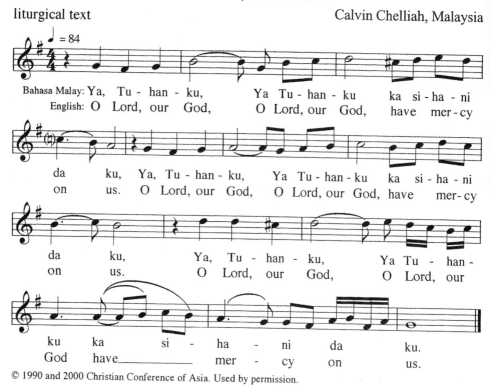

Bahasa Malay: Ya, Tu-han-ku, Ya Tu-han-ku ka si-ha-ni
English: O Lord, our God, O Lord, our God, have mer-cy

da ku, Ya, Tu-han-ku, Ya Tu-han-ku ka si-ha-ni
on us. O Lord, our God, O Lord, our God, have mer-cy

da ku, Ya, Tu-han-ku, Ya Tu-han-
on us. O Lord, our God, O Lord, our

ku ka si-ha-ni da ku.
God have mer-cy on us.

33

Zhu a! qiu
Lord, have mercy

liturgical text

Lu Chen Tiong, Malaysia

Mandarin: Zhu a! qiu ni lian min wo.
(translit.)
English: Lord, have mer - cy on us.

Ji du qiu ni lian min wo.
Christ, have mer - cy on us.

Zhu a! qiu ni lian min wo.
Lord, have mer - cy on us.

Kyrie

Gracious Lord, have mercy

34

liturgical text

Piret Pormeister-Rips, Estonia

Kyrie

Lord, have mercy

35

liturgical text

Dinah Reindorf, Ghana

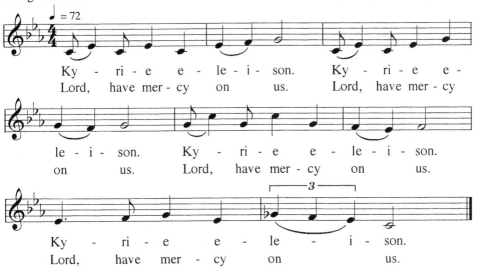

36 Santo, santo, santo
Holy, holy, holy
(Sanctus)

Isa 6:3, Matt. 21:9
Eng. para., Jorge Lockward

folk song, Peru

Ritmo de Marinera ♩. = 80

Estribillo/Refrain

Spanish: San - to, san - to, san - to, san - to es el Se - ñor. San - to, san - to, san - to, san - to es el Se - ñor.

English: Ho - ly, ho - ly, ho - ly, ho - ly is our God. Ho - ly, ho - ly, ho - ly, ho - ly is our God.

Last time to Coda

1. Hos - san - na en las al - tu - ras, ben - di - to el nom - bre de Dios.
2. A - lé - gren - se cie - lo y tie - rra en Cris - to, Dios Sal - va - dor.

1. Ho - san - na in the high - est, blessed be the name of our God.
2. Let heav - en and earth re - joice in Christ Je - sus, Re - deem - ing God.

D. C. al Coda *Coda*

ñor.
God.

Thooyaa, thooyaa, thooyare 37
Holy, holy, holy
(Sanctus)

Isa. 6:3, Matt. 21:9

M. Thomas Thangaraj, India

Tamil: (translit.) Thoo - yaa, thoo - yaa, thoo - ya - re!
English: Ho - ly, ho - ly, ho - ly Lord,

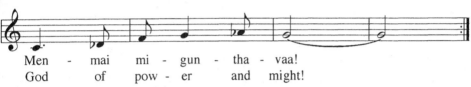

Men - mai mi - gun - tha - vaa!
God of pow - er and might!

Vin - nil im - man - nil en - gum um maan - be
Heav - en and earth are full of your glo - ry.

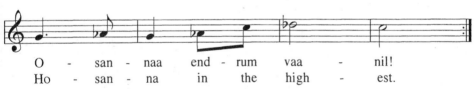

O - san - naa end - rum vaa - nil!
Ho - san - na in the high - est.

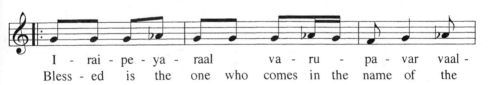

I - rai - pe - ya - raal va - ru - pa - var vaal -
Bless - ed is the one who comes in the name of the

ga O - san - naa end - rum vaa - nil!
Lord. Ho - san - na in the high - est.

38

Aandavar thaam
Christ has died
(Memorial Acclamation)

M. Thomas Thangaraj, India

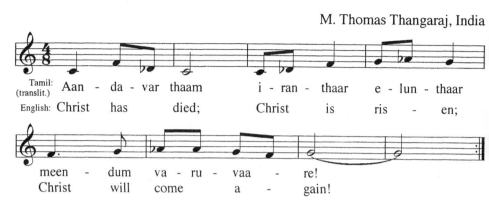

Tamil: (translit.) Aan - da - var thaam   i - ran - thaar   e - lun - thaar
English: Christ   has   died;   Christ   is   ris - en;

meen - dum   va - ru - vaa - re!
Christ   will   come   a - gain!

39

Amen

M. Thomas Thangaraj, India

A - - men,   a - - men,

a - - - - - - men.

Du är helig
You are holy

words and music, Per Harling, Sweden

Part 1* (may be sung as a canon)

Swedish: Du är he - lig, Du är hel,
English: You are ho - ly, you are whole,

Du är all - tid myck - bar mer, än vi
you are al - ways ev - er more than we

nån - sin kan för - stå. Du är nä - ra än - då.
ev - er un - der - stand, you are al - ways at hand.

Väl - sig - nad va - re Du. Som
Bless - ed are you com - ing near, bless - ed

41 Holy, holy, holy Lord
(Sanctus, Red Lake)

Isa. 6:3, Matt. 21:9

Monte Mason after melodies found in
Chippewa Music by Frances Densmore

Leader: Ho-ly, ho-ly, ho-ly Lord

All: Ho-ly, ho-ly, ho-ly Lord

Gi-chi Ma-ni-doo, / God of pow'r and might, heav-en and earth are full of your glo-ry.

Ho-san-na in the high-est.

Bless-ed is the one who comes in the name of the Lord. Ho-san-na in the high - - - est.

42 Amen

Chinese folk melody
arr., Puqi Jiang, China

♩ = 96

A - men, a - men, a - - men.

A - men, a - men, a - - men.

Woman live a Moab lan'

(Ruth and Naomi)

43

Barry Chevannes, Jamaica

arr. Patrick Prescod

1. Wo - man live a Mo - ab lan'__ __ your name, _____ name Ruth, name Ruth. Wo - man live a Mo - ab lan'_____ name Ruth, name Ruth. Ruth loved Na - o - mi
2. Pret - ty la - dy tell me what_ - ter Ruth, what your name? Pret - ty la - dy tell me what your name, what your name? Me name Ruth, a
3. Gwan back home me daugh- - son from back home. Gwan back home me daugh - ter Ruth, gwan back home. Fin' your - self an -
4. Broth - ers, sis - ters, learn a les - son from the book of love. Broth - ers, sis - ters, learn a les - son from the book of love. Ruth love Na - o - mi

44 En la Escritura encontramos
God's Holy Word has provided
(Tu palabra es luz)

words and music, Eleazar Torreglosa, Colombia
Eng. trans., S T Kimbrough, Jr.

Porro colombiano ♩ = 88

Spanish: En la Es-cri-tu-ra en-con-tra-mos luz pa-ra nues-tro ca-
English: God's Ho-ly Word has pro-vid-ed light for the way we are

mi - no, nos guí - a por don-de an-da - mos
go - ing; a - long our path - way we're guid - ed;

pa - ra mar-car el des - ti - no En la Bi-blia
des - ti-ny's seed it is sow - ing. We have in the

lla - mos ma-nan - tial de vi - da,
Bi - ble springs of liv - ing wa - ters,

45

Au preah vo bey
Our Father, who is in heaven

Matthew 6:9-13
Khmer translit., Lenita Tiong

Barnabas Mam, Cambodia
harm., Carlton R. Young

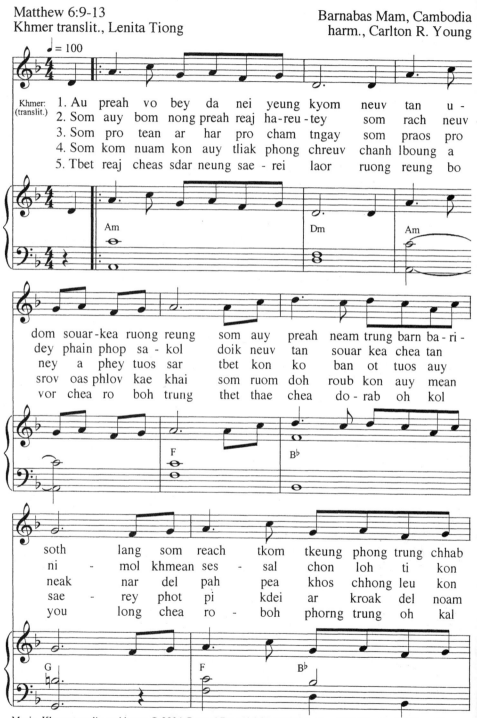

Khmer:
(translit.)

1. Au preah vo bey da nei yeung kyom neuv tan u-
2. Som auy bom nong preah reaj ha-reu-tey som rach neuv
3. Som pro tean ar har pro cham tngay som praos pro
4. Som kom nuam kon auy tliak phong chreuv chanh lboung a
5. Tbet reaj cheas sdar neung sae-rei laor ruong reung bo

dom souar-kea ruong reung som auy preah neam trung barn ba-ri-
dey phain phop sa-kol doik neuv tan souar kea chea tan
ney a phey tuos sar tbet kon ko ban ot tuos auy
srov oas phlov kae khai som ruom doh roub kon auy mean
vor chea ro boh trung thet thae chea do-rab oh kol

soth lang som reach tkom tkeung phong trung chhab
ni - mol khmean ses - sal chon loh ti kon
neak nar del pah pea khos chhong leu kon
sae - rey phot pi kdei ar kroak del noam
you long chea ro - boh phorng trung oh kal

mork　　　　dol.
leng　　　　nar.
rual　　　　thngai.
sao　　　　morng.

chea　nik　A - men.

Dm　　　　　　Dm　　Bb/D　　Dm

Our Father, who is in heaven　46
Au preah vo bey

Matthew 6:9-13
Eng. para., S T Kimbrough, Jr.

Barnabas Mam, Cambodia

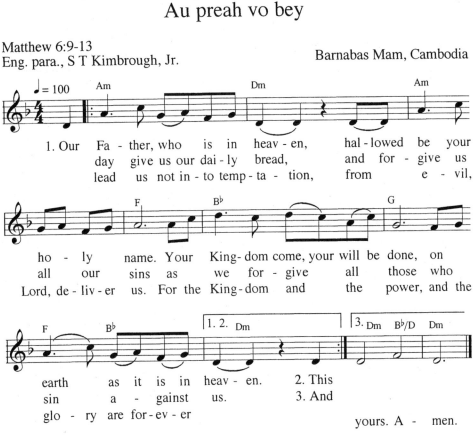

♩ = 100　Am　　　　　　　　Dm　　　　　　　　Am

1. Our　Fa - ther, who　is　in　heav - en,　hal - lowed　be　your
day　give us our dai - ly　bread,　　　and　for - give　us
lead　us not in - to temp - ta - tion,　from　　　e - vil,

F　　　　Bb　　　　　　　　　　G

ho - ly　name. Your　King- dom come, your will be done,　on
all　our　sins　as　we　for - give　all　those who
Lord, de - liv - er　us. For the King- dom　and　the　power, and the

F　　　Bb　　　　1. 2. Dm　　　　3. Dm　Bb/D　Dm

earth　as　it　is　in　heav - en.　2. This
sin　a - gainst　us.　3. And
glo - ry　are for - ev - er　　　　yours. A - men.

47 Temesgean Eyesus
Thank you, Jesus

trad. song, Ethiopia

harm., Carlton R. Young

Amaric: 1. Te - mes - gean E - ye - sus. Te - mes - gean E - ye - sus.
2. Ewe - da - ha - leu Eye - sus. Ewe - da - ha - leu Eye - sus.

English: 1. Thank you, thank you, Je - sus, thank you, thank you, Je - sus,
2. Praise you, praise you, Je - sus, praise you, praise you, Je - sus,

Te - mes - gean E - ye - sus be - le - be.
Ewe - da - ha - leu Eye - sus be - le - be.

thank you, thank you Je - sus, in my heart.
praise you, praise you, Je - sus, in my heart.

Te - mes - gean E - ye - sus. Te - mes - gean E - ye - sus.
Ewe - da - ha - leu Eye - sus. Ewe - da - ha - leu Eye - sus.

Thank you, thank you, Je - sus, thank you, thank you, Je - sus,
Thank you, thank you, Je - sus, thank you, thank you, Je - sus,

Te - mes - gean E - ye - sus be - le - be.
Ewe - da - ha - leu Eye - sus be - le - be.

thank you, thank you, Je - sus, in my heart.
thank you, thank you, Je - sus, in my heart.

Come to the Supper

48

Patrick Matsikenyiri, Zimbabwe
transcr., Mark McGurty

Charles Wesley, Great Britain

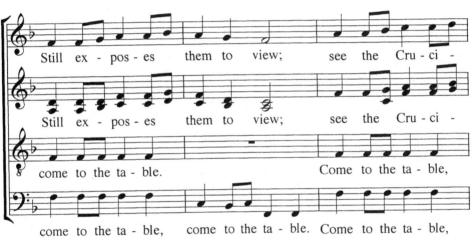

T. Come to the ta - ble, come to the ta - ble, come to the ta - ble.

B. Come to the ta - ble, come to the ta - ble, come to the ta - ble,

Come to the ta - ble, come to the ta - ble,

come to the ta - ble. Come to the ta - ble, come to the ta - ble,

come to the ta - ble,

come to the ta - ble, come to the ta - ble.

Performance note: The soprano and alto parts may be sung without the tenor and bass parts, beginning at line 2 on the first page and concluding at the last measure of the third page. Shakers and drums may also be added as rhythm instruments.

1. Come to the Supper, come,
    sinners there still is room;
   every soul may be his guest,
    Jesus gives the gen'ral word.
   Share the monumental feast,
    eat the Supper of your Lord.

2. In this authentic sign
    behold the stamp divine.
   Christ revives his sufferings here,
    still exposes them to view;
   see the Crucified appear,
    now believe he died for you!

Hymns on the Lord's Supper (1745).

Hindi ko maisip

Far beyond our mind's grasp
(What a great mystery)

49

Francisco F. Feliciano, Philippines

Bicol folk song
arr. Francisco F. Feliciano

Pilipino:
1. Hin - di ko ma - i - sip, kay la - king hi -
2. Ang a - bang ling- kod mo'y di ka - ra - pat -
3. Nang a - king ma - la - sap a - lak at tin -
4. Sa - na'y sa pag - li - san, sa i - yong ta -

wa - ga___ Kay la - king pag - li - ngap,
da - pat___ Sa - yo'y ma - ki - sa - lo,
a - pay___ A - king ka - ga - la - kan
ha - nan___ A - ming mga pu - so ay

pag - pa - pa ka - sa - kit,_____ Sa - la na - ming
ma - ki - pag-ha - pu - nan,_____ Di na nag - na -
ay wa - lang ma - pag-si - dan_____ Di ki - na-kai -
i - yong lu - ku - ban_____ Na-mag - ing dam -

ta - o nang i - yong a - ku - in_____
na - is ng ma - ra - ming ba - gay_____
lang - ang a - kin pang wa - ri - in_____
ba - na ng iyong ka - bu - ti - han_____

_____ Wa - lang hang - ga - nan, Diyos, ang 'yong pag - i -
_____ Sa - pat na ma - da - ma'ng i - ka'y ka - pi -
_____ Kung ba - kit ang li - ga - ya ko'y wa-lang pa -
_____ Mag - ing hu - wa - ran ng pag - ma - ma-ha -

big.
ling.
tid.   lan.

Far beyond our mind's grasp $\mathbf{50}$
Hindi ko maisip
(What a great mystery)

Bicol folk song
arr. Francisco F. Feliciano

Francisco F. Feliciano, Philippines

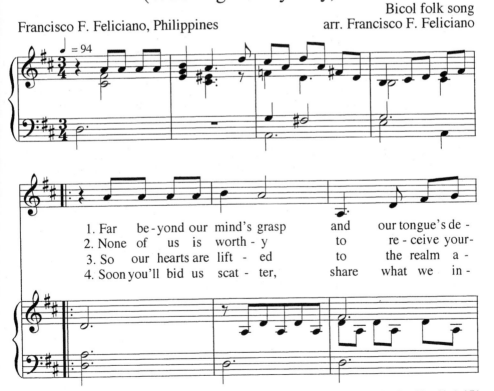

1. Far   be-yond our mind's grasp   and   our tongue's de -
2. None of   us is   worth - y   to   re - ceive your-
3. So   our hearts are lift - ed   to   the realm a -
4. Soon you'll bid us scat - ter,   share what we in-

O God, how won-der-ful! You call us through the veil.
your prom-ise is for life; we on-ly can re-joice.
we thank you for this feast, this fel-low-ship div-ine.
to light the lamps of those who al-so seek your face.

A va de laa mioo

Come, one and all

51

words and music, Billema Kwillia, Liberia

Loma:
1. A va de laa mi-oo, dii-oo, a va de laa mi-oo, dii-oo, a de Zii-ze lɔ-tɔi mi-oo, dii-oo.
2. A va de boa-le-oo, dii-oo, a va de boa-le-oo, dii-oo, a de Zii-ze may-mai boa-ieo, dii-oo.
3. Gá sa ni-i-ni bu, dii-oo, gá sa ni-i-ni bu, dii-oo, da sa Zii-ze nii-ni bu-oo, dii-oo.
4. A va de laa mi-oo, dii-oo, a va de laa mi-oo, dii-oo, a de Zii-ze lɔ-tɔi mi-oo, dii-oo.

52 Come, one and all
A va de laa mioo

words and music, Billema Kwillia, Liberia
Eng. para., S T Kimbrough, Jr.

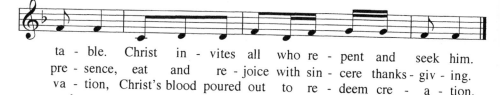

1. Come, one and all, to the ta - ble, come one and all to the
2. Here eat the bread of Christ's pre - sence, here eat the bread of Christ's
3. Here drink the cup of sal - va - tion, here drink the cup of sal-
4. Rise now, pro-claim-ing the good news, rise now, pro-claim-ing the

ta - ble. Christ in - vites all who re - pent and seek him.
pre - sence, eat and re - joice with sin - cere thanks - giv - ing.
va - tion, Christ's blood poured out to re - deem cre - a - tion.
good news: The ris - en Christ has re - deemed cre - a - tion.

53 Viešpatie, tu atpirkai
Through your holy blood

author unknown
Eng. trans., Kristin Markay

trad. melody, Lithuania
harm., Carlton R. Young

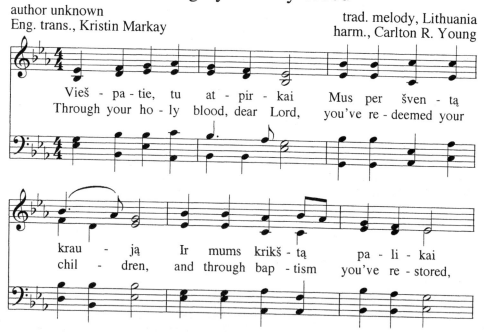

Vieš - pa - tie, tu at - pir - kai Mus per šven - tą
Through your ho - ly blood, dear Lord, you've re - deemed your

krau - ją Ir mums krikš - tą pa - li - kai
chil - dren, and through bap - tism you've re - stored,

At - gim - dyt iš nau - jo, Nuo mir - ties ir
claimed and loved us once a - gain. From dark death and

nuo kan čiu Plauk tą kū - di - kė - lį Ir gai - vi - nan -
suf - fer - ings, wash this ti - ny in - fant and with your re -

čiu žo - džiu Šven - tink ma - žu - tė - lį.
new - ing words bless the life you've giv - en.

Khwaam suk yeun

Happy the ones

54

SRI LAMPANG
trad. melody, Thailand

Ps. 1

1. Khwaam suk yeun yong khong maa suu phuu tham chop,
2. Dai khwaam cham roen phloet phloen jit reun cheun baan,
3. Faay thaang khon chua haa pen dang chen nan mai,
4. Kit kaan khon chua yawm wi - bat yuaei yap pai

phuu kawb duai jai man nai sat thaa
meuan phreuk tra kaan rim thaan pliam chon
meuan klaeb kra jaay taam saay lom phaa
tham wai yaang rai yawm dai - kae - ton

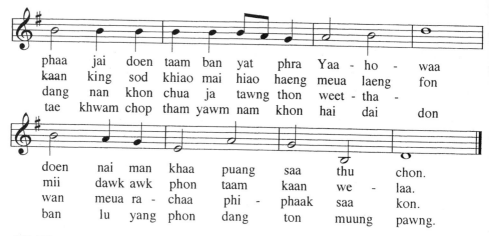

phaa jai doen taam ban yat phra Yaa - ho - waa
kaan king sod khiao mai hiao haeng meua laeng fon
dang nan khon chua ja tawng thon weet - tha -
tae khwam chop tham yawm nam khon hai dai don

doen nai man khaa puang saa thu chon.
mii dawk awk phon taam kaan we - laa.
wan meua ra - chaa phi - phaak saa kon.
ban lu yang phon dang ton muung pawng.

55   Happy the ones
Khwaam suk yeun

Ps. 1, Eng. para., Erik Routley

SRI LAMPANG
trad. melody, Thailand

1. Hap - py the ones who walk in God's wise way,
2. Theirs is the life where du - ty and de - light
3. Fret - ful and anx - ious are the sin - ners' days,
4. Lord, in your mer - cy spare me, keep me still,

hap - py who shun the sin - ful choice:
nour - ish each oth - er bliss - ful - ly;
bar - ren and lone - ly is their path;
let me not choose the sin - ner's way;

hap - py who find their pleas - ure in God's law,
as when be - side a broad and gen - erous stream
like wind on dust the judg - ment of the Lord
prom - ise and law you e - qual - ly have given:

hap - py who heed God's right - eous voice.
proud - ly stands ev - er - green the tree.
scat - ters their pride in sud - den wrath.
Let them be my de - light to - day.

I love the Lord

Isaac Watts, Great Britain
Ps. 116:1-2

Richard Smallwood, USA
arr., Nolan Williams, Jr.

1. I love the Lord,_____
2. I love the Lord,_____

— he heard my cry   and pit-ied
— he heard my cry   and chased my

57
Cantai ao Senhor
Rejoice in the Lord

Ps. 98:1
Eng. para., C. Michael Hawn

trad. melody, Brazil
arr., Simei Monteiro

Portuguese: Can-
English: Re-

tai ao Se - nhor um cân - ti - co no - vo, can-
joice in the Lord and sing God a new song; re-

tai ao Se - nhor um cân - ti - co no - vo, can-
joice in the Lord and sing God a new song. Re-

tai ao Se - nhor um cân - ti - co no - vo, can -
joice in the Lord and sing God a new song. Re -

tai ao Se -nhor, can - tai ao Se - nhor. Can -
joice, let us sing. Re - joice, let us sing. Re -

2. Porque ele fez, ele fez maravilhas. (3x) For God's holy arm has gained us the vic'try.
   Cantai ao Senhor, cantai ao Senhor.   Rejoice, let us sing, rejoice, let us sing.

3. É ele quem dá o Espírito Santo.   (3x) Give thanks to our God, who gave us the Spirit.
   Cantai ao Senhor, cantai ao Senhor.   Rejoice, let us sing, rejoice, let us sing.

4. Jesus é o Senhor! Amem, aleluia! (3x) For Jesus is Lord! Amen, alleluia.
   Cantai ao Senhor, cantai ao Senhor.   Rejoice, let us sing, rejoice, let us sing.

58 K go ram vozvozhu vzory
I lift up my eyes to the hills

Ps. 121
Russian translit., William Lovelace

Juri Pasternak, Russia

1. K go ram voz-vo-zhu vzo-ry mah-yee: ot-ku-da pri-dyot po-mozh' ka mnye? Ot Bo-ga pri-dyot po-mozh' ka mne, ot Tvor-
2. Sto-pa tva-yah pust' nye pryet knyot-cya vah-vyek I pust' nye us-nyot chra-nee-tyel tvahyee! on nye zad-ryem lyet, i nye us-nyot, nye us-
3. Chra-neet tyeb-ya Bog, pok-rov nad tah-boi, pok-rov nad ta-boi, nad dyes-nee tzey tva-yee. I nye pov-rye-deet tye-bye soln-tze vah dnee, I lu-
4. Gos-pod sach-ra-neet ot vsya-ko-vo zla, Gos-pod sakh-ra-neet du-shu tva-yoo, svaee vi-chod i vchod, do-ro-gee tva-ee sach-ra

Refrain

tza nye - byes i zyem - li. A - do - nai,
nyot, kyem Eez - ra - eel' chra - neem.
na nye kas - nyot - cya v no - chee.
neet vah vye - kee ve - kov.

al - le - lui - ya, al - le - lui - ya, A - do - nai!

A - do - nai, al - le - lui - ya,

al - le - lui - ya, A - do - nai!

59 I lift up my eyes to the hills
K go ram vozvozhu vzory

Ps. 121, Eng. para., S T Kimbrough, Jr.   Juri Pasternak, Russia

1. I lift up my eyes to hills a - bove. From whence comes my help? It comes from God, the Ma - ker of heaven, Ma - ker of earth, for
2. Your God nev - er sleeps, your Sen - ti - nel; God will not per - mit your foot to slip. The Keep - er of Israel, God slum - bers not, for
3. Your Keep - er is God and is a shade, up - on your right hand; by day the sun will do you no harm, nor moon by night, for
4. The Lord is your shield from e - vil's power, pro - tects your own soul for ev - er - more, your com - ing and going, all of your ways, are

Refrain

God sus-tains all life. A - do - nai, al -le - lu -ia,
God sus-tains all life.
God sus-tains all life.
ev - er in God's care.

al - le -lu - ia, A - do - nai! A - do - nai,

al - le - lu - ia, al - le - lu -ia, A - do - nai!

60 Lord, I will lift mine eyes
(Total Praise)

words and music, Richard Smallwood, USA

arr., Stephen Key

Lord, I will lift mine eyes to the hills

know - ing my help is com - ing from you.

Your peace you give me in time of the storm.

You are the source of my strength.

You are the strength of my life. I lift my

61 O God, you search me

based on Ps. 139
words and music, Bernadette Farrell

1. O God, you search me and you know me. All my thoughts lie o - pen in your gaze. When I walk or lie down you are be - fore me: Ev - er the

2. You know my rest - ing and my ris - ing. You dis - cern my pur - pose from a - far, and with love ev - er - last - ing you be - siege me: In ev - ery

3. Be - fore a word is on my tongue, Lord, you have known its mean - ing through and through. You are with me be - yond my un - der - stand - ing: God of my

4. Al - though your Spir - it is up - on me, still I search for shel - ter from your light. There is no - where on earth I can es - cape you: E - ven the

5. For you cre - at - ed me and shaped me, gave me life with - in my moth - er's womb. For the won - der of who I am, I praise you: Safe in your

maker and keeper of my days. 2. You
moment of life or death, you are. 3. Be -
present, my past, and future, too. 4. Al -
darkness is radiant in your sight. 5. For
hands, all creation is made new.

Naega sanŭl hyanghayŏ 62
To the high and kindly hills

Song-suk Im, Korea
Ps. 121

Song-chon Lee, Korea

♩. = 60 Taegum (flute)

Kayagum (zither)

Chang-go (drum)

Korean: (translit.) Nae - ga san - ŭl hyangha-yŏ   nun - ŭl dŭ - ne
English: To the high and kind-ly hills   I   lift   my eyes;

na-ŭi do-um-i ŏ-di-sŏ o-nŭn - ga
where is some-one to res-cue me in my plight?

na-ŭi do-um-i ch'ŏn-ji-rŭl ji ŭ - shin.
Tru-ly from the dear Lord a-bove help will come.

Yŏ-ho-wa ha-na-nim-e-ge-sŏ o - ne.
God is the Mak-er of heaven and earth: all is well.

Create in me a clean heart

63

words and music, George Mulrain, Trinidad and Tobago
Ps. 51:1-3, 10, 11

arr. Leslie Mowatt

Cre - ate in me a clean heart, O God, and re -
new a right spir - it with - in me.
Cast me not a - way from your pres - ence and
take not your Spir - it from me. Have mer cy up-
from all my

on me, O God, ac - cord - ing to your stead - fast
in - iq - ui - ty, cleanse me thor - ough - ly from my

love; ac - cord - ing to you're a - bun - dant
sin. For I ac - knowl - edge all my trans -

mer - cy and blot out all my sins_____
gres - sions and my un -

Cleanse me end - ing sins.

64 Mikoron Dávid
David, the king

Mihály Vég, Hungary
after Ps. 55

Zoltán Kodály, Hungary

Hungarian:
1. Mi - ko - ron Dá - vid nagy bú - sul - tá - ban, ba - rá - ti mi - att
2. Is - te - nem U - ram kér - lek én té - ged, for - dít - sad re - ám
3. Te a - zért, lel - kem, gon - do - la - to - dat, Is - ten - be ves - sed

vol - na bá - nat - ban, pa - na - szol - kod - ván nagy ha - rag - já - ban,
szent sze me - i - det: Nagy szük - sé - gem - ben ne hagyj en - ge - met,
bi - zo - dal - ma - dat: Ró - lad el - vé - szi min - den ter - he - det

I - lyen kö - nyör - gést kez - de ó ma - gá - ban:
mert meg - e - mész - ti nagy bá - nat szí - ve - met.
És meg - hall - gat - ja te kön - yör - gé - si - det.

David, the king

65

Mikoron Dávid

Mihály Vég, Hungary, after Ps. 55
Eng. trans., S T Kimbrough, Jr.

Zoltán Kodály, Hungary

1. Da - vid, the king, was once so frustrat-ed; friends made him ang - ry
2. My Lord, my God, O hear now my yearning; please hear the prayer with-
3. Take heed, my soul, with trust as you're plead-ing, God is the One who

and ir - ri - tat - ed. His sharp com-plain-ing was an - i - mat-ed,
in me that's burn-ing: Let now your eyes, Lord, to me be turn-ing,
knows what you're need - ing. God takes your cares; O, fol-low his lead-ing;

till from his soul a prayer em-an - at - ed.
change my dis-stress to in - ner dis-cern - ing.
God's ev - er pre-sent, God's in - ter-ced - ing.

66 Bueno es alabarte, Señor
God, how wondrous to give you our praise

words and music, Pedro Ortiz, Costa Rica
Ps. 92
Eng. trans., S T Kimbrough, Jr.

harm., Jorge Lockward

♩ = 96

Spanish: 1. Bue - no es a - la - bar - te, Se - ñor y a tu
2. Son tus o - bras ex - cel - sas, Se - ñor, y es pro -

English: 1. God, how won - drous to give you our praise, and our
2. When I think of your works, I'm spell - bound, and your

nom - bre fol - clo - res can - tar; de ma - ña - na tu
fun - do tu e - ter - no pen - sar, el que es ne - cio no

voic - es in folk - songs to raise, in the morn - ing to
e - ter - nal thoughts, how pro - found! Of your pow'r fools say,

gra - cia a - nun - ciar y de no - che tu fi - de - li -
ve tu po - der y el que pe - ca ig - no - ra tu a -

sing of your grace, and at night of your strong faith - ful -
"God can't be found" and their sin ig - nores e - ven your

dad. Con las seis cuer - das del gui - ta - rrón
mor. Aun - que a - bun - den las o - bras del mal
ness. With the strings of the grand gui - ta - rrón,
love. And though e - vil ones' works mul - ti - ply

— y ma - rim - bas de rít - mi - co son pues tus
— y cual hier - ba naz - ca el pe - ca - dor, a la
— and ma - rim - bas' own rhyth - mi - cal tone, O what
— and their growth like the grass pro - phe - cy what they

he - chos me a - le - gran, Se - ñor, son tus o - bras mi
rui - na sus o - bras i - rán, por - que tú e - res el
joy in your deeds I have shown, and the works of your
do fin - al - ly turns to ruin, be - cause you are the

fe - li - ci - dad. El jus - to flo - re - ce
San - to Se - ñor.
hands make me glad. The just flour - rish and they
one ho - ly God.

Estribillo/Refrain

Pesnata na radosta

When you waken in the morning

67

words and music, Gordana Miteva, Macedonia
Eng. para., S T Kimbrough, Jr.
Macedonian translit., Robert Milcev

arr., Robert Milcev

♩ = 122

Macedonian: (translit.)
1. V tvoj-te o - chi gled - am ra - dost ne mo -
2. Bo - ze na - pra - vi ne do - bri Tvo - jot

English:
1. When you wak - en in the morn - ing, does God
2. Lord, now grant to us your Spir - it, fill us

zam da ve - ru - vam ka - ko to - a da se slu -
duh von as da e vra - ti ni ja ra - do - sta_

know your ev - ery need, as you start the day re - joic-
with sal - va - tion's joy. Let the goal to be your wit-

- chi sve - to da go o - sta - vish. Jas znam kje sve -
__ na na - she - to Spa - se - ni - e kje sve -
- ing and you turn to God to plead? When you
- ness - es each hour our souls em - ploy. Then we'll

68 Al despuntar en la loma el día
When o'er the hills

words and music, Heber Romero, Cuba
from *La Liturgia Criolla*

arr. Jorge Lockward

Spanish:
1. Al des - pun - tar en la lo - ma el dí - a,
2. Se mez - cla el sol en el ho - ri - zon - te
3. Qui - sie - ra ser co - mo a - quel a - rro - yo,

al ver tu glo - ria na - cer,
con un ver - de ca - fe - tal,
gra - to pa - ra re - fres - car

te ve -o a -quí, co -mo siem - pre, en mi
y tú me pi -des que can - te, y te
mi voz se al -za en el vien - to, oh mi

D   A

vi - da   y en mi ser;
can - to,   mi Se - ñor;
Dios, pa -   - ra can - tar;

Bm   E   A   A⁷

te ve -o a -quí, co -mo siem - pre, en mi
y tú me pi -des que can - te, y te
mi voz se al -za en el vien - to, oh mi

D   A

vi - da   y en mi ser.
can - to,   mi Se - ñor.
Dios, pa -   - ra can - tar.

Bm   E⁷   A   E

When o'er the hills

Al despuntar en la loma el día

69

words and music, Heber Romero, Cuba
from *La Liturgia Criolla*
Eng. trans., S T Kimbrough, Jr.

arr. Jorge Lockward

1. When o'er the hills morn-ing light is break - ing,
2. On the ho - ri - zon the sun is blend - ing
3. I want to be like a brook that's flow - ing;

once more your glo - ry is born.
with hues of green cof - fee fields,
O how re -fresh - ing, such grace!

Filled with your joy all the fields are wak - ing
and from the bush there's a bird - song wend - ing
Or like the sound of a soft wind blow - ing—

and grow - ing grass greets the morn.
till it a new life re - veals.
your thoughts through palm groves I'd trace.

A dif -ferent day now is dawn - ing
The air with fra - grance is swell - ing,
I hear the roos - ter that's crow - ing,

and yet, with fear, I am torn;
a sweet a - ro - ma I smell.
the thrill -ing bird - song takes wing!

70 Burung murai tela
Bird calls announce the morning

author unknown, Indonesia

Irian Jaya melody
transcr. Hanoch Tanatty

Bahasa
Indonesia:
1. Bu - rung mu-rai te - la ber - nya-nyi ri - ang,
2. Fa - jar te-rang ter-bit meng - u - sir si - ang,
3. Ka - mi ter-ban-gun da - ri ti-dur pu - las,

Tan - da ma-lam a-kan di - gan-ti si - ang
dan ke-ge-la-pan do-sa - pun ter-be-nam,
dan men-ik-ma-ti ka-sih tak ter-ba-las,

Ya Tu - han Al - lah, Ra - ja se - mes - ta,
Kris - tus Tu - han Fa-jar ke - bang-ki - tan,
Ya Tu - han men-ta - ri ke - ben - a - ran,

Pa - da-Mu sa - ja ka - mi ber - se - rah.
su - dah meng-a-lah-kan ke - ma - ti - an.
A - nug'-rah-kan ka-mi peng - ha - ra - pan.

Bird calls announce the morning 71
Burung murai tela

author unknown, Indonesia
Eng. trans. Hanoch Tanatty, alt.

Irian Jaya melody,
transcr. Hanoch Tanatty

♩ = 88-96

1. Bird calls an-nounce the morn-ing with joy-ful song.
2. Sun-rise dis-pels the dark-ness and fears of night;
3. Sleep's death-like spell is bro-ken when birds are heard,

This is a sign that day's here and night is gone.
sin's prince, pre-fers the sha-dows, de-tests the light:
once more we wake to God's grace and lov-ing Word.

Teach us your hand-i-work, Lord, to pon-der.
Christ rose from death to new life be-fore dawn,
O Christ, you are the true Sun of heav-en,

O sov'-reign God, we bow down in won-der.
sang how your Spir-it freed him, Earth's First-born.
shine rays of peace a-mong us for ev-er.

72 Kiedy ranne wstaja zorze

In the distance day is breaking

Fr. Karpinski, Poland

trad. melody, Poland
arr., T. Kiewice

Polish:
1. Kie - dy ran - ne wsta - ją zo - rze, To - bie zie - mia,
2. Led - wie oc - zy prze - trzeć zo - dłam, wnet do me - gô
3. Wie - lu snem śmier - ci up - ad - li, co się wczo - raj

To - bie mo - rze, To - bie spie - wa ży - wioł wszel - ki:
Pa - na wo - łam, Do me - go Bo - ga na nie - bie
spać pok - ła - dli, My się jesz - cze o - bud - zi - li,

Bądź po - chwa - lon, Bo - że wiel - ki!
i szu - kam Go ko - ło sie - bie.
boś - my cię Bo - że, chwa - li - li.

In the distance day is breaking 73
Kiedy ranne wstaja zorze

Fr. Karpinski, Poland
Jeffrey Myers, alt.

trad. melody, Poland
arr., T. Kiewice

1. In the dis - tance day is break - ing, earth and sea glad
2. Lord, be - fore you I am stand - ing, your hand grasp - ing,
3. Friends who walk with us no long - er, held by death, yet

sounds are mak - ing. All cre - a - tion joins in sing - ing,
love ex - pand - ing, your own dwell - ing I will en - ter,
love is strong - er. Day dawns bright, new hope ex - tend - ing,

God, to you thanks - giv - ing bring - ing.
you, my God, are my life's cen - ter.
thanks to God in praise un - end - ing.

74 Por la mañana
I waken each new day

words and music, Alfredo Colom, Guatemala
Eng. trans., S T Kimbrough, Jr.

Spanish: Por la ma-ña-na yo di-ri-jo mi a-la-ban-za
English: I wa-ken each new day with joy and ju-bi-la-tion,

a Dios que ha si-do y es mi ú-ni-ca es-pe-ran-za.
for God a-lone's my source of glad-ness and e-la-tion.

Por la ma-ña-na yo le in-vo-co con el al-ma
My soul cries out, "O God, give us new in-spi-ra-tion!

y le su-pli-co que me dé su dul-ce cal-ma.
O bring us peace!" a prayer for ev-ery gen-er-a-tion.

75 Kaugel väljal helisevad kellad

Can't you hear the distant bells

Heli Viht, Estonia
Eng. trans., Kristin Markay

Piret Pormeister-Rips, Estonia

Estonian: Kau - gel väl - jal he - li - se - vad kel - lad,
English: Can't you hear the dis - tant bells are ring - ing?

nen - de ku - min kos tab ü - le maa.
Peo - ple wak - en as they hear their song.

O - rus, o - ja kal - dal ha - jub u - du,
Ev - ery - where the air is filled with mu - sic.

ter - ve maa võib jäl - le är - ga - ta.
Now we see a new day has be - gun.

päev, mis mei - le kor - du - ma - tu, uus.   Ol - gu
God has giv - en us a brand - new day.   We're re -

sel - lel päe - val me pla - nee - dil
joic - ing for this new be - gin - ning.

kõik - jal ra - hu, rõõm ja va - ba - dus.
Cel - e - brate this Eas - ter gift to - day.

Maye komm na mehwe

I will quietly wait on the Lord

76

words and music, A. E. Amankwah, Ghana
Eng. trans., alt.

arr., Hartmut Bietz

Twi: Ma - ye komm na meh - we On - ya - me. Ma - ye
English: I will qui - et - ly wait on the Lord. I be -

komm na meh - we On - ya - me. Ma - ye
lieve what is said in God's word: "I'll re -

komm na meh - we On - ya - me. Ma - ye
new your strength as you pray." Then I'll

komm na meh - we On - ya - me. Ma -
fly with wings like a bird. I'll

ye se a - ba - fra wa wo no. Ma - ye komm na meh -
be just like a new - born babe; I will qui - et - ly

1.
we On - ya - me.
wait on the Lord.

2.
Ma - we On - ya - me.
I'll wait on the Lord.

77

Pasibaigė diena
The day is at an end

words and music, Agnė Laurinaitytės, Lithuania
Eng. para., S T Kimbrough, Jr.

Pa -si -bai -gė die - na jau Die -vas ke - ti - na už- deg-
The day is at an end, God's set - ting the stars in the sky_

- ti vi - sas žvaigž - des dan - gu - je. Ber-
__ as the child - ren kneel at their beds. Their

niu - kai, mer - gy - tės klau - pias prie lo - vy - tės, o
guard - i - an an - gels stand at their side, hov' - ring a -

an - ge - lai sto - vi jų ša - ly - je._
round their heads. I can sleep and be calm;_

Ga - liu ra - mai mie - go ti
I dream of you, of you,_

a - pie ta - ve sap - nuo - ti, nes tu taip ar - ti__
be -cause you're stand - ing near me. Now I pray: For - give_

78

Oseh Shalom
May the Source of Peace

from the Kaddish prayer,
Sanctification of God,
Jewish Liturgy

Nurit Hirsch, Israel
arr., Mary Feinsinger

*Alternative texts appear within brackets.

79

Pokea moyo wangu
Receive my soul

trad. mourning hymn, Kenya
Eng. trans., Bilha Adagala Pfukani
adapt., S T Kimbrough, Jr.

trad. melody, Kenya
arr. Patrick Matsikenyiri, Zimbabwe

Swahili: Po - ke - a mo - yo wa - ngu e Mu - ngu wa -
English: Re - ceive my soul, I pray, O God, re - ceive my

ngu ni - we - ze ku - ku - pen - da kwa pen -
soul; that I may love you, Lord my God, for

do la - ko U - ni - pe mo - yo
your love's sake. Your heart, dear God, now

wa - - ko e - we Ye - su mko -
give me. A - bide with me, O

mbo - zi wa - ngu shi - nda kwa - ngu na -
Je - sus Christ, my Sa - vior; I'll a -

Fine

mi da - i - ma kwa - - ko.
bide with you for ev - - - er.

O - nye - ni muo - ne kwa - mba Bwa - na yu mwe -
O taste and see that God, the Grac - ious One, is

ma. He - ri yu - le um' - tu a -
good, and bless - ed are those who

D. C. al Fine

na - ye mtu - ma - i - ni Ye - su Kri - sto.
put their trust in Je - sus Christ.

80 'Eiki Mafimafi
Lord God Almighty

trad. benediction, Tonga
Eng. trans., Sione Tu'uta

VESPERS
Federick A. Mann

'Ei - ki ma - fi - ma - fi ta - li 'e - mau hu. 'O - mi ha ke-
Lord God Al - migh - ty, hear us now, we pray. Clothe us in your

le - si, to - ka ha - mo - nu. Ka mau tu - tu - ku 'Ei - ki
grace, Lord, bless - ed be your name. As we leave this place, Lord,

tau tu - tu - ku mu'a fai a tu 'a e fe - ohi,
lead us forth, we pray; may we have for ev - er

o tu - pu - tu - pu'a. 'E - me - ni.
fel - low - ship in faith. A - men.

Na Jijoho

May the God of peace be with you

81

trad. words and music, Benin
Eng. trans., S T Kimbrough, Jr.

arr., Geoff Weaver
adapt., Carlton R. Young

Na Ji-jo-ho, ji - jo-ho ni tin. Na Ji-jo-ho,
May the God of peace and of all good, may the God of

ji - jo-ho ni tin. Po ome - po - po. A -
peace and of all good be al -ways with you. A -
ome - po - po. A -
be with you. A -

men. Po ome - po - po. A - men!
men; may God's peace be with you. A - men!
men, ome - po - po. A - men!
men, be with you. A - men!

82

Gospodi pomilui
Lord, have mercy on us

Peter Dinev, Bulgaria

Gos - po - di po - mi - lui, Gos - po - di po - mi - lui,
Lord, have mer - cy, have mer-cy on us.

Gos-po-di po-mi - lui, Gos - po-di po-mi - lui,
Lord, have mer - cy, have mer - cy, O Lord, on us.

Gos - po-di po-mi - lui, Gos - po - di po-mi - lui,
O Lord, have mer-cy on us, O Lord, have mer-cy on us.

Te - be Gos - po - di. A - min.
have mer - cy, Lord, on us. A - men.

83

Salamun Kullaheen
May peace be with you

author unknown

folk melody, Lebanon

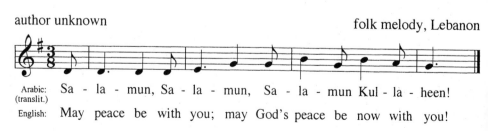

Arabic: Sa - la - mun, Sa - la - mun, Sa - la - mun Kul - la - heen!
(translit.)

English: May peace be with you; may God's peace be now with you!

Lord of life, we come to you **84**

ERISKAY LOVE LILT
trad. Scots Gaelic tune
arr., *Common Ground*, eds.

Catherine Walker

1. Lord of life, we come to you. Lord of
2. Through the days of doubt and toil, in our

all, our Sav - ior be. Come to bless and to
joy and in our pain, guide our steps in your

heal with the light of your love.
way, make us one in your love.

We pray to you, O God **85**

Ivor H. Jones, UK

We pray to you, O God, Fa - ther, Son, and Spir- it.

86 Lajahle, htaora Hp'ya
Come, O come, let us praise

University Christian Fellowship, Myanmar

Saw Gideon Tun Shwe,
Myanmar

1. La - jah - le, hta - o - ra Hp'ya, hta - o - ra
2. La - jah - le, Kri - taw Hp'ya Kri - taw
3. La - jah - le, wing - iñ Hp'ya wing - iñ

1. Come, O come, let us praise Par - ent
2. Come, O come, let us praise Christ, our
3. Come, O come, let us praise Spir - it

Hp'ya i mye-ta-daw ko - chi - moañ zoh-ley,____
Hp'ya i Je-zu-daw ko - chi - moañ zoh-ley,____
Hp'ya i mye-tha ha-yah ko - chi - moañ zoh-ley,____

God, O praise the love of God, the great I Am,____
King, O praise the grace of Christ, the Prince of Peace,____
God, the fel-low-ship of Ho - ly Spir - it God,____

—— mye - ta - daw ko - chi - moañ zoh - ley.
—— Je - zu - daw ko - chi - moañ zoh - ley.
—— mye - tha ha - yah ko - chi - moañ zoh - ley.

—— praise the love of God, the great I Am.
—— praise the grace of Christ, the Prince of Peace.
—— fel - low-ship of Ho - ly Spir - it God.

Sara shriste
You are author and Lord

87

words and music, Kiran Kumar Pradhan, Nepal
Nepali translit., Devi and Karuna Bhujel

harm., Carlton R. Young

Nepali: (translit.) Sa - ra shri -sti - ka ma - lik ta - pa -im-lain Sa - ra
English: You are au - thor and Lord of cre - a - tion; you are

shri - sti - ka ra -shaka ta - pa -im-lain Ha - mro
mak - er of life and of liv - ing. And from

hri - daya sa - me-ta - le a - dar -pra - nam sa-
deep in our hearts won - der and love in-

88 Perëndi plot madhështi
God of all the universe

words and music, Valentin Veizi, Albania

Albanian:
1. Pe - rën - di plot ma - dhë - shti, kri - jo - ve Ti hap'- sir''pa - fund, dhe za - mba - kun plot me ves'_ e shpir - tin tim që drit' kë - kon.
2. Je - zus të fa - lë - nde - roj që n'rru - gën e gjat' me plot mun - dim mu - a më kër - ko - je Ti,_ të fshe - hur në më - ka - tin tim.
3. E në fund më - gje - te Ti, më - zgja - te do - rën e' gja - ko - sur, do - rën ti - me fort shtrën - go - ve dhe a - to ku - rrë më s'u ndan'.

Refrain

Fa - lem nder, fa - lem nder, fa - lem' - nder - it Zot, fa - lem' - nder - it o Zot.

Fa - lem nder, fa - lem nder, fa - lem' - nder - it Zot, fa - lem' - nder - it, o Zot.

God of all the universe

Perëndi plot madhështi

89

words and music, Valentin Veizi, Albania
Eng. trans., S T Kimbrough, Jr.

1. God of all the u - ni - verse, Cre - a - tor of
2. Je - sus, you a - lone I thank; for me, my
3. I re - joice you found me, God, your wound - ed

all: heav - en and earth; you made flow - ers gleam with dew,
God, you suf - fered pain, and your gra - cious love sought me
hand stretched out to me. Then you grasped my hand with yours

— you made my soul that seeks your light.
— when weight - ed down by bur - d'ning sin.
— and now from you noth - ing can sev - er.

Refrain

I give thanks, I give thanks, I give thanks to our

God. I give thanks, thanks to our God.

— I give thanks, I give thanks, I give thanks to our

God. I give thanks, thanks to our God.

© 1997 V. U. SH. Rr. "Fadil Rada," 143 Tiranë. Eng. trans. © 2004 General Board of Global Ministries, GBGMusik, 475 Riverside Dr., New York, NY 10115. All rights reserved.

90

Boh náš je láska
Love is eternal

words and music, Maria Royová, Slovakia

Slovak:
1. Boh náš je lás - ka od več - nos - ti, On zá - klad
2. Boh náš je lás - ka od več - nos - ti, On pra - men
3. Boh náš je lás - ka od več - nos - ti, On dar - ca
4. Boh náš je lás - ka od več - nos - ti, no neu - zri-

by - tia, prúd mi - lo - sti. Z lá - sky vy - tvo - ril,
ši - ly, lúč svet-lo - sti. Do rú - cha krá - sy
syä - tej bla - že-nos - sti. Z lá - sky vy - ku - pil
eš ho bez svä-to - sti. Ó, v ěa - ro - kras - ny,

zdr - žu - je svet. Kde nie-to Je - ho, ži - vo - ta niet!
ob - lie -ka svet! Kde nie-to Je - ho, ra - dos - ti niet!
stra - te -ný svet, Kde nie-to Je - ho, spa - se - nia niet!
nadh-viez-dny svet, bez rú-cha slá - vy prís - tu - pu niet!

Boh náš je lás - ka, Boh náš je lás - ka!

Love is eternal
Boh náš je láska

91

words and music, Maria Royová, Slovakia
Eng. para., S T. Kimbrough, Jr.

♩ = 110

1. Love is e - ter - nal, for God is love. All the cre-
2. Love is e - ter - nal, for God is love. All God's cre-
3. Love is e - ter - nal, this now we know. Through Christ, the
4. God is e - ter - nal, this now we see. Seek God, find

a - tion by love does move. All that we are and
a - tion good - ness does prove. Al - pha, O - me - ga,
door, God's bless - ings o'er - flow. He is our free - dom,
love, and what's yet to be. God is a - mong us

all we can be lies in God's pow - er e - ter - nal - ly.
God we a - dore. God's will a - lone knows what is in store.
truth and our light. Through Christ, sal - va - tion gives us new sight.
not just a - bove. There is no fu - ture with - out God's love.

Love is e - ter - nal; God is e - ter - nal.

Eng. para. © 2004 General Board of Global Ministries, GBGMusik, 475 Riverside Dr., New York, NY 10115.
All rights reserved.

92 O Ségnè, nou pòté rémèsiman
Loving God, we come with thanks

Marco Dépestre, Haiti

George Mulrain, Trinidad and Tobago

Haitian Creole:

1. O Sé - gnè, nou pò - té ré - mè - si - man pou biin - fè Ou ki an - pil: Ou fè tè pé - yi nou a trè fè - til Pou pa man - ké a - li - man. O Bon Pa - pa! O Bon Pa - pa! Pi - tit ou yo rann ou gloua! A - lé - lou - ya! A - lé - lou - ya! A - lé - lou - ya!

2. O ga - dé ki biin - fè Bon - Dieu ban nou: Nou jouinn ré - kolt san kon - prann Sak pa - sé nan pié ka - fé, poua, ban - nann, nan pié flè nou ouè pa - tou. A la mè - vèy! A la mè - vey! A la Bon - Dieu Bon Pa - pa!

3. Min Dieu di: Pin sèl pa kab bay la vi Gnou lè nou pap man - jé, bouè. Li vlé prann souin nou i - sit sou la tè Pou nou viv nan Jé - zu - Kri. O pran ké nou! O pran ké nou! Bon Pa - pa ki rin - min nou!

Loving God, we come with thanks 93
O Ségnè, nou pòté rémèsiman

Marco Dépestre, Haiti
Eng. trans., George Mulrain

George Mulrain, Trinidad and Tobago

♩ = 120

Am | Bb | C7 | F | F

1. Lov - ing God, we
2. See the wond' - rous
3. God said: Not by

Bb | F | Bb | C

come with thanks o'er - flow - ing, grate - ful for your gifts so free:
har - vest God has giv - en. It is such a my - ste - ry:
bread a - lone that I give, may you live up - on the earth;

F | Bb | F | Bb | F

You cre - a - ted this our fer - tile coun - try that we'll not lack
cof - fee, peas, ba - na - na, ev - ery fruit tree, flow' - ring plant that
my de - sign was through the Sav - ior Christ's birth all for him would

C7 | F | C | F | C7

an - y - thing. Great Cre - a - tor! Great Cre - a - tor!
points to heav'n. Great and marv' - lous! Great and marv' - lous!
learn to live. God, re - ceive us, God, ac - cept us!

F | Am | Bb | C | F

Prais - es come from near and far! Al - le - lu - ia!
God, you are so good to us.
Thanks for your great love to us.

Bb | Am | Bb | C7 | F

Al - le - lu - ia! Al - le - lu - ia!

94 Sithi bonga
We sing praise

words and music, George A. Mxadana, South Africa
Eng. para., S T Kimbrough, Jr.

arr., Patrick Matsikenyiri

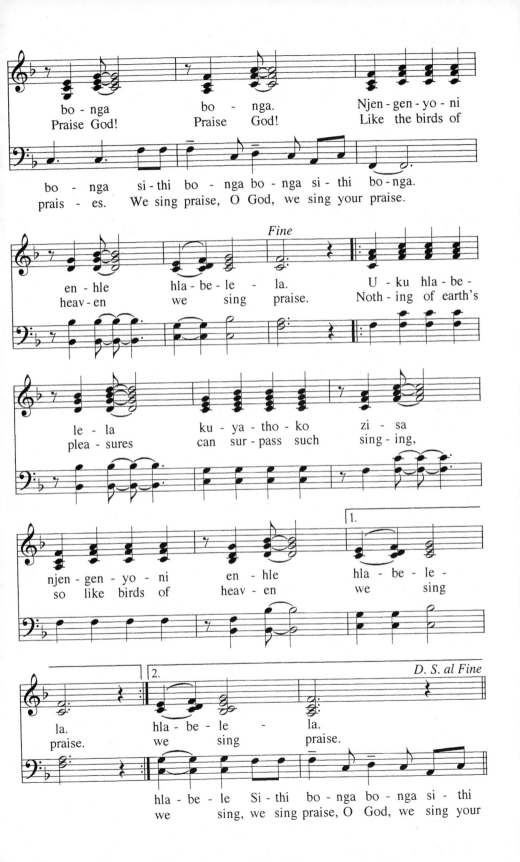

95 More than we know

Shirley Erena Murray, New Zealand

Lu Chen Tiong, Malaysia
based on Malay folk motives

1. More than we know, God works with-
2. He is God's eye, chang - ing our
3. He is God's face, smile of the
4. He is God's heart, tuned to our

in us, more than we trust,
fo - cus, he is the light,
rain - bow, co - lor of peace,
heart - beat, he is the air, *simile*

mus - tard seeds grow, more than we dream,
flood - ing our mind, he is the fire,
blend - ing us all, he is the coin,
lift - ing our wings, his are the arms

God's pos - si - bil - i - ty, this is the gos - pel of
Spir - it and en - er - gy spark - ing our spir - it to
God's new e - con - o - my, spend - ing to feed and to
stretched out, to chal - lenge us, he is our cour - age to

Refrain

love: for Christ has come bring - ing us life,
shine,
save,
fly,

Christus ist unser Friede
Jesus Christ is our freedom
96

Horst Krüger, Germany
Eng. trans., S T Kimbrough, Jr.

Guillaume Franc
Johann Crüger

97 Jesus, Savior, Spirit, Sun

Shirley Erena Murray, New Zealand

Swee-Hong Lim, Singapore

1. Je - sus, Sav - ior, Spir - it, Sun!
2. Blind and scat - tered, we have gone
3. One by one, the walls have grown
4. Je - sus Christ, con - sume our shame

You the life that makes us one.
seek - ing cross - es of our own,
in tra - di - tions set like stone,
in the love which is your flame,

Melt us, fuse us in your fire,
build - ing church - es not the Church,
stub - born walls of hu - man pride
Je - sus, Sav - ior, Spir - it, Sun,

mold   us   to   your   heart's   de - sire.
ghet - to - mind - ed   in   our   search.
built   to keep the   Christ out - side.
you   the   life that makes us   one.

Koi au na sala na dina 98
I am the Way

John 14:6
Eng. trans., S T Kimbrough, Jr.

trad. melody, Fiji

Fijian: Koi au na sa - la na di - na na bu - la,
English: "I am the Way, the Truth and the Life,"

ka - ya ko Ji - su.   Se - ga na sa - la e - da na
that's what Je - sus said.   With - out the Way there's no way

se - se,   se - ga na di - na e - da na we - le, se - ga na
to go; with - out the Truth there's no way to know. And with - out

bu - la e - da na ru - sa.   Koi au na sa - la na
Life there's no way to live.   "I am the Way, the

di - na na bu - la,   ka - yo ko Ji - su.
Truth and the Life,"   that's what Je - sus said.

99

Hinge nsenge
I will praise my Lord

Justin Baransa, Burundi

1. Hi - nge hi - nge; Hi - nge
2. Hi - gne ndi - rim - be, Ndi - rim -
3. Nzo - mu - ko - re - ra, Nko - re -

1. I will praise my Lord, I will
2. I will sing for him, songs of
3. I will serve my Lord, I will

1. Je bé - nis Jé - sus, Jé bé -
2. Je chante pour lui, chants de
3. Je lui o - bé - is, je tra -

1. nse - nge U-mwa - mi wa - nje hi - nge.
2. be uwo Mwa - mi ari we Ye - su.
3. re uwo Mwa - mi ari we Ye - su.

1. praise my Lord and Sav - ior Je - sus.
2. praise I'll sing for my Lord Je - sus.
3. al - ways be his faith - ful ser - vant.

1. nis Jé - sus, mon sau - veur Jé - sus.
2. gloi - re pour mon sau - veur Jé - sus.
3. vai - lle pour mon sau - veur Jé - sus.

Refrain

D. C.

Ya - mpa - ye vyi - nshi: Hi - nge nse - nge hi - nge. Ya-
Ur' a - ma ho - ro: Hi - nge nse - nge hi - nge. Ur'
Ur' ur - u - ku - ndo: Hi - nge nse - nge hi - nge. Ur'
N'u - mu - we - ze - ro: Hi - nge nse - nge hi - nge. N'u
N'u - mwi - de - gem - vyo: Hi - nge nse - nge hi - nge. N'u

He gave me all I have, I'll praise my Sav - ior. He
He gave me peace with God: I'll praise my Sav - ior. He
He gave me love for all: I'll praise my Sav - ior. He
He gave me per - fect joy: I'll praise my Sav - ior. He
He set me free from sin: I'll praise my Sav - ior. He

Il m'a don - né la vie, Jé - sus m'a sau - vé. Il
Il m'a don - né la paix, Jé - sus m'a sau - vé. Il
Il m'a don - né l'a - mour, Jé - sus m'a sau - vé. Il
Il m'a don - né la joie, Jé - sus m'a sau - vé. Il
Le Christ m'a li - be - ré, Jé - sus m'a sau - vé. Le

*After each stanza, sing all five lines of the refrain.

Music, Eng. trans., French trans. © 1987 All Africa Council of Churches. Source: *L'Afrique Chante*.

Let us enter into covenant 100

words and music, Norbert Farrell, St. Vincent

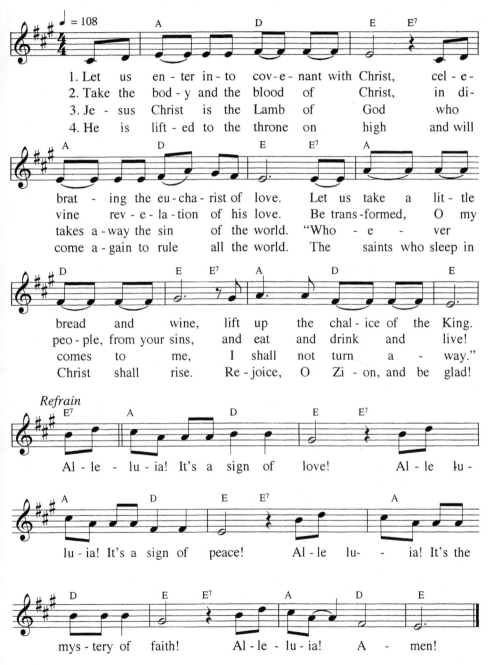

1. Let us en - ter in - to cov - e - nant with Christ, cel - e-
2. Take the bod - y and the blood of Christ, in di-
3. Je - sus Christ is the Lamb of God who
4. He is lift - ed to the throne on high and will

brat - ing the eu - cha - rist of love. Let us take a lit - tle
vine rev - e - la - tion of his love. Be trans - formed, O my
takes a - way the sin of the world. "Who - e - ver
come a - gain to rule all the world. The saints who sleep in

bread and wine, lift up the chal - ice of the King.
peo - ple, from your sins, and eat and drink and live!
comes to me, I shall not turn a - way."
Christ shall rise. Re - joice, O Zi - on, and be glad!

Refrain

Al - le - lu - ia! It's a sign of love! Al - le - lu-

lu - ia! It's a sign of peace! Al - le - lu - ia! It's the

mys - tery of faith! Al - le - lu - ia! A - men!

101 Man Jėzaus vardas
The name of Jesus Christ

Richardas Lupas, Lithuania/Germany

S T Kimbrough, Jr., USA
harm., Mary K. Jackson

1. Man Jė - zaus var - das toks, gra - žus, Jis
2. Jis sti - pri - na pa - var - gu - sius, Ra -
3. Kad siau - čia au - dros, aš tvir - tai Ga -
4. Jis ve - da ma - ne vi - sa - da Ir

skam - ba ma - lo - niai, Kiek - vie - no tik - in -
mi - na jų šir - dis; Jis at - gai - vi - na
liu ant Jo sto - vėt, Kad nyk - sta jė - gos
už - ta - ria mei - liai. Jei aš suk - ly - dęs,

čio jaus - mus Jis pa - ke - lia auk - štai.
ken - čian - čius Ir ke - lia jų vil - tis.
man vi - sai,— Ga - liu į Jį ti - kėt.
Jis ta - da Vis iš - ve - da tik - rai.

The name of Jesus Christ **102**
Man Jėzaus vardas

Richardas Lupas, Lithuania/Germany
Eng. trans., S T Kimbrough, Jr.

S T Kimbrough, Jr., USA
harm., Mary K. Jackson

♩ = 110

1. The name of Je - sus Christ re - sounds with love for
2. The faint with strength our Lord re - vives, calms ev - ery
3. When storms pre - vail and bil - lows roll, my course on
4. O Christ, my ev - er faith - ful guide, with love di -

hu - man - kind. Though pain with - in my
trou - bled heart. Through him the suf - fering
Christ is stayed. When I'm a weak - ened,
rect my way; and should I fall, be

heart a - bounds, in Christ I heal - ing find.
soul sur - vives, through hope, the heaven - ly art.
down - cast soul, through faith I'm not a - fraid.
at my side— my con - stant strength and stay.

103 Svete tichi svjatyje
Jesus Christ, Joyous Light

words and music from the Russian Orthodox liturgy
Eng. trans., R. Birch Holye

arr. Hartmut Bietz

Sve - te ti - chi svja - ty - je sla - vy bes -
Je - sus Christ, Joy - ous Light! pure ray from the

smert - na - go Ot - ca ne bes - na - vo, svja -
blaz - ing splen - dor of the Fa - ther, who

ta - go bla žen - na - go I - i - su - se Chris-
dwells im - mor - tal, hal - lowed, blest, in heav - en a -

te; pri - šed - še na za - pad soln - ca, vi -
bove! Once more we come at sun - set hour; while

dev - še svet ve - čer - nij, po - jem Ot -
cheer - ful lamps give glad - ness a - mid the

ca, Sy - na i svja - ta - go Du - cha Bo -
gloom, one God we praise, Fa - ther, Son and Ho - ly

ga. Do - sto - in je - si vo vsja vre - me -
Ghost. To you, Ev - er - last - ing Son of the

na pet by ti gla - sy pre - po - dob - ny -
Fa - ther, sa - cred an - thems ev - er should we

mi, Sy - ne Bo - žij, žy - vot - da -
sing: you are wor - thy of all

jaj: tem - že mir tja sla - vit.
wor - ship, you have brought e - ter - nal life.

Percussion patterns for "Njoo kwetu, Roho mwema," 104,
and "Gracious Spirit," 105.

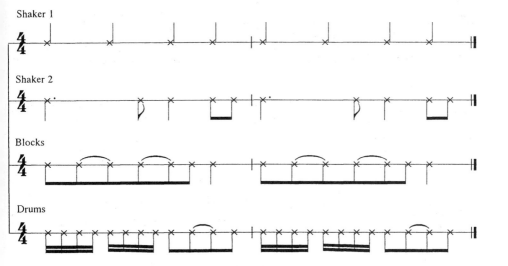

Shaker 1

Shaker 2

Blocks

Drums

104 Njoo kwetu, Roho mwema
Gracious Spirit

Wilson Niwagila, Tanzania

Ganda Melody, Tanzania
arr., C. Michael Hawn

Swahili:
1. Njo-o kwe-tu, Ro-ho mwe-ma, M-fa-ri-ji we-tu. Tu-fu-ndi-she ya mbi-ngu-ni, tu-we wa-tu wa-pya. Njo-o, njo-o, njo-o, Ro-ho mwe-ma.
2. Ut-fa-ny-e wa-a-mi-ni wa Ye-su Mwo-ko-zi. Tu-ka-i-shi ki-ku-ndi-ni, ka-ni-sa-ni mwa-ko.
3. Kwa nu-ru-ma tu-ba-ri-ki, tu-i-shi na we-we. Tu-ka-te-nde ki-la ki-tu ku-o-ngo-zwa na-we.
4. Ro-ho mwe-ma M-fa-ri-ji, u-tu-pe he-ki-ma; Tu-ki-wa-za na ku-te-nda, yo-te ya-we ya-ko.
5. Tu-du-mi-she tu-we ha-i na u-kwe-li wa-ko. Tu-si-vu-twe na du-ni-a, tu-shu'-die ne-e-ma.

Refrain

Gracious Spirit
Njoo kwetu, Roho mwema

105

Wilson Niwagila, Tanzania
trans., Howard S. Olson

Ganda Melody, Tanzania
harm., C. Michael Hawn

1. Gra-cious Spir-it, heed our plead-ing, fash-ion us all a-new. It's your lead-ing that we're need-ing, help us to fol-low you. Come,
2. Come to teach us, come to nour-ish those who be-lieve in Christ. Bless the faith-ful, may they flour-ish, strength-ened by grace un-priced. Swahili: Njo - o,
3. Guide our think-ing and our speak-ing done in your ho-ly name. Mo-ti-vate all in their seek-ing, free-ing from guilt and shame.
4. Not mere knowl-edge, but dis-cern-ment, nor root-less lib-er-ty; turn dis-qui-et to con-tent-ment, doubt in-to cer-tain-ty.
5. Keep us fer-vent in our wit-ness; un-swayed by earth's al-lure. Ev-er grant us zeal-ous fit-ness, which you a-lone as-sure.

come, come, Ho-ly Spir-it, come.
njo - o, njo - o, Ro-ho mwe-ma.

106 Sheng ling ru feng
Holy Spirit, you're like the wind

words and music, Wei-fan Wang, China
Mandarin translit., David Wu

harm., Guo-ren Zhong

Mandarin:
(translit.)

1. Sheng ling ru feng, feng he ru? Dan wen feng sheng zhi tou guo, feng guo zhi tou hao hua kai, sheng ming hua kai feng chui chu, chang chui
2. Sheng ling ru chuan ching shan lu, huo zuo qi liu huo fei bao, huo zuo chiang he yu yu chi, huo shui zhi yün, shu chang lu. Zhi yün
3. Sheng ling ru yu chang jiao zhu, yu man deng chan kuang man wu, yu cuo gao yu man yi chin, sheng ai xing xiang xiang fu you, chang ciao
4. Sheng ling ru jian she dao fu, bo kai ling huen ji jing gu. Wo zhu xuan mu ru lie yuan, dong cha ren xing yi fei fu, jian cha
5. Sheng ling ru huo ran yung lu, lian wo lu zhong fo zha chu. Yu ru da kuang zao cheng du, xing yuan ming liang wu mi wu. Ran shao

Words and music © 1983, 1999 by China Christian Council. Used by permission. Mandarin translit. © 2004 General Board of Global Ministries, GBGMusik, 475 Riverside Dr., New York, NY 10115.

107 Holy Spirit, you're like the wind

Sheng ling ru feng

words and music, Wei-fan Wang, China
trans., Grace Shangjuan, alt.
Ivy Balchin and W. H. Wong, alt.

harm., Guo-ren Zhong

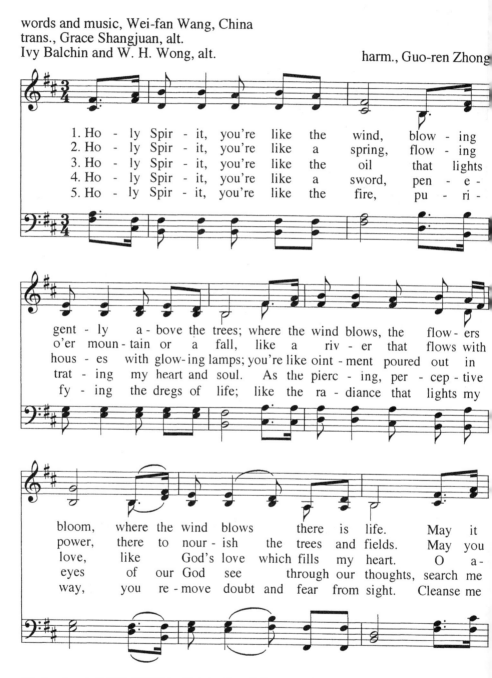

1. Ho - ly Spir - it, you're like the wind, blow - ing gent - ly a - bove the trees; where the wind blows, the flow - ers bloom, where the wind blows there is life. May it
2. Ho - ly Spir - it, you're like a spring, flow - ing o'er moun - tain or a fall, like a riv - er that flows with power, there to nour - ish the trees and fields. May you
3. Ho - ly Spir - it, you're like the oil that lights hous - es with glow-ing lamps; you're like oint - ment poured out in love, like God's love which fills my heart. O a -
4. Ho - ly Spir - it, you're like a sword, pen - e - trat - ing my heart and soul. As the pierc - ing, per - cep - tive eyes of our God see through our thoughts, search me
5. Ho - ly Spir - it, you're like the fire, pu - ri - fy - ing the dregs of life; like the ra - diance that lights my way, you re - move doubt and fear from sight. Cleanse me

blow, O blow or'e me; I pray that it
rich - ly nour - ish me; that I may bear
noint me, pour on me, bathe me in God's
God. O God, search me. For - give my hid -
God, O God, cleanse me, guide me to path -

shall nev - er cease. Ho - ly Spir - it, you bring the
fruit a - bun - dant - ly; ev - er bear - ing the fruits of
grace, my on - ly hope. Teach me al - ways, O Ho - ly
den i - ni - qui - ties. In your light, God, I'm stripped com -
ways of your love. Make me, God, your own bea -

spring - time, like mut - ed flowers fra - grance out - pour.
life, that de - pend on life - giv - ing dew.
Spir - it, and I will lis - ten and o - bey.
plete - ly, mould me in your im - age as you wish.
con, your light a - bid - ing, a flame of love.

108 Öffne meine Ohren
Open now my ears

author unknown

Wolfgang Fürlinger, Austria

1. Öff - ne mei - ne Oh - ren, Hei - li - ger Geist,
2. Öff - ne mei - ne Au - gen, Hei - li - ger Geist,
3. Öff - ne mei - nen Geist, Hei - li - ger Geist,
4. Öff - ne mei - nen Mund, Hei - li - ger Geist,
5. Öff - ne mei - ne Hän - de, Hei - li - ger Geist,
6. Öff - ne mein Ge - müt, Hei - li - ger Geist,

damit ich deine Bot - schaft hö - re.
damit ich die Schönheit der Schöp - fung se - he.
damit ich deine Bot - schaft glau - be,
damit ich deiner Herrlichkeit Zeug - nis ge - be.
damit ich deine Hil - fe fas - se.
damit ich deine Nä - he lie - be.

7. Öff - ne mein Herz, öff - ne mein Herz, Hei - li - ger Geist,

da - mit ich dei - ne Lie - be spü - - re.

da - mit ich dei - ne Lie - be spü - re.

Open now my ears

Öffne meine Ohren

author unknown
Eng. trans., S T Kimbrough, Jr.

Wolfgang Fürlinger, Austria

109

1. O - pen now my ears, Spir - it of God,
2. O - pen now my eyes, Spir - it of God,
3. O - pen now my spir - it, Spir - it of God,
4. O - pen now my mouth, Spir - it of God,
5. O - pen now my hands, Spir - it of God,
6. O - pen now my sen - ses, Spir - it of God,

that I may hear your mes - sage.
that I may see the beauty of your cre - a - tion.
that I may re - ceive your mes - sage.
that I may witness to your splen - dor.
that I may receive your as - sist - ance.
that I may love your near - ness.

7. O - pen my heart, o - pen my heart, Spir - it of God,

that I may feel your love, feel your___ love.

that I may feel your love, feel your love.

110 Afio mai, Agaga Sa e
Come, Holy Spirit, in this hour

trad. hymn, Samoa

transcr., Carlton R. Young

Samoan:
1. A - fi - o mai, A - ga - ga Sa e, I le - nei i - tu - la, Ma fa'a - ma - la - ma - la - ma mai, I lo - to po - gi - sa.
2. Ua fa'a - po - u - li - u - li - gia, Ma fa' - se - se - ina ai; Ua le i - loa se fi - a fia Ua ma - tu - a vai - vai.
3. Le - nei ia o - fa - o - fa - tai, Ma fo - ai i - na mai, se lo - to fou ia te i ma - tou Ia ma - tou le - lei ai.

Come, Holy Spirit, in this hour 111
Afio mai, Agaga Sa e

trad. hymn, Samoa
Eng. para., S T Kimbrough, Jr.

transcr. Carlton R. Young

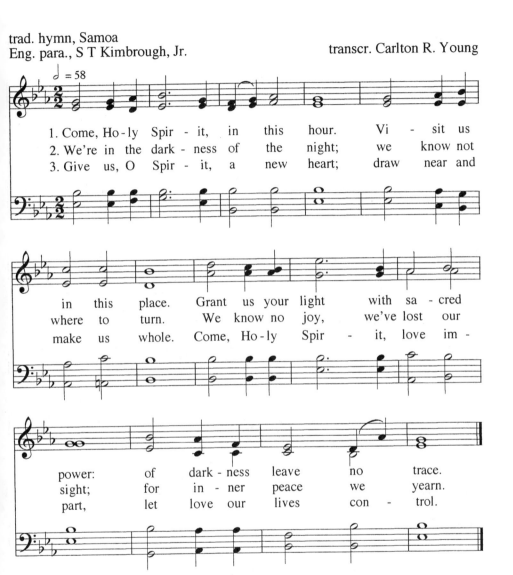

1. Come, Ho-ly Spir - it, in this hour. Vi - sit us
2. We're in the dark - ness of the night; we know not
3. Give us, O Spir - it, a new heart; draw near and

in this place. Grant us your light with sa - cred
where to turn. We know no joy, we've lost our
make us whole. Come, Ho-ly Spir - it, love im -

power: of dark - ness leave no trace.
sight; for in - ner peace we yearn.
part, let love our lives con - trol.

Eng. para. and music transcr. © 2004 General Board of Global Ministries, GBGMusik, 475 Riverside Dr., New York, NY 10115.

112 Esprit, toi qui guides
Good Spirit of God

Didier Rimaud, France

Jean van der Cauter, Belgium

French: 1. Es - prit, toi qui gui - des tous les hom - mes,
2. Es - prit, toi qui souf - fles sur le mon - de,
3. Es - prit, toi que don - nes la jus - ti - ce,

gar - de - les pour la gloi - re du
brû - le - nous de ta flam - me si
don - ne - nous de com - bat - tre la

Pè - re; u - nis - les dans ton peu - ple de la
clai - re; pur - i - fie tous nos ges - tes de mi -
hai - ne; for - ce - nous à dé - fen - dre ceux qui

ter - re; con - duis - les par la rou - te qui
sè - re; con - duis - nous où la grâ - ce du
pein - ent, con - duis - nous vers les pau - vres qui

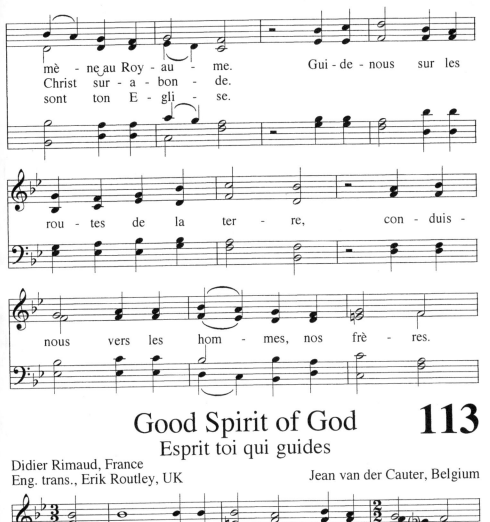

mè - ne au Roy - au - me. Gui - de - nous sur les
Christ sur - a - bon - de.
sont ton E - gli - se.

rou - tes de la ter - re, con - duis -

nous vers les hom - mes, nos frè - res.

Good Spirit of God 113
Esprit toi qui guides

Didier Rimaud, France
Eng. trans., Erik Routley, UK

Jean van der Cauter, Belgium

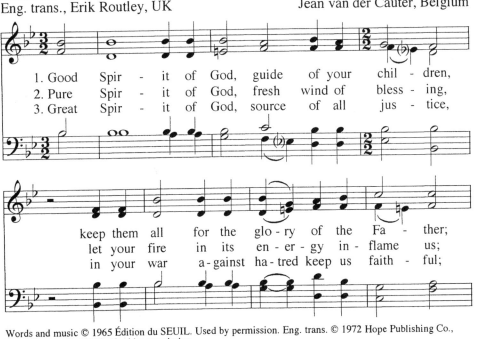

1. Good Spir - it of God, guide of your chil - dren,
2. Pure Spir - it of God, fresh wind of bless - ing,
3. Great Spir - it of God, source of all jus - tice,

keep them all for the glo - ry of the Fa - ther;
let your fire in its en - er - gy in - flame us;
in your war a - gainst ha - tred keep us faith - ful;

keep them all   in the love of one an - oth - er;   lead them
let your heal - ing from mis - er - y re - claim us;   lead us
in pro - tect - ing the poor keep us watch - ful;   in our

all   in the   quest   for the   hon - or   of the   King - dom.
all   where the   faith - ful Christ's grace   are con - fess - ing.
search   for the   house - hold of   peace   still pro - tect   us.

Be our guide through this pil - grim - age of liv - ing,

turn us   each   to each   oth - er   in self - giv - ing.

Elolo nye Mawu

God loves me

words and music, Togo and Ghana
Eng. para., S T Kimbrough, Jr.

Mawu = "Ma-u"; elolo = open "o" as in "knock"; dzi = dsi

115 Herra, kädelläsi asua mä saan
God, your hands enfold me

Anna-Mari Kaskinen, Finland

Pekka Simojoki, Finland

Finnish:
1. Her-ra, kä-del-lä-si a-su-a mä saan,
Siel-lä kaik-ki saa-vat uu-den sy-dä-men,
2. Her-ra kä-del-lä-si i-loi-ta mä saan,
Siel-lä ar-mah-du-sta meil-le tar-jo-taan.
3. Her-ra kä-del-lä-si it-ke-ä mä saan,
Si-tä nau-lat pis-ti pa-huus ih-mis-ten

tur-val-li-sin kä-si pää-lä maan.
rau-han an-nat haa-vat si-to
se on ri-kas kä-si an-ta-maan.
ei-kä ka-do-tus-ta mil-loin-
ko-hon-nut ei kä-si kos-ta-maan.
an-teek-si soi ris-ti kai-ken

116 God, your hands enfold me

Herra, kädelläsi asua mä saan

Anna-Mari Kaskinen, Finland
trans., Per Harling, alt.

Pekka Simojoki, Finland

1. God, your hands en - fold me, faith - ful - ly I live
   Ev - ery heart that's bro - ken, ev - ery wound - ed soul
2. God, your hands en - fold me, when I pray to you,
   Re - con - ciled, for - giv - en, once and yet a - gain:
3. God, your hands en - fold me in my woe - ful cry
   God, you con - quer e - vil through your Son's own pain,

Dm C B♭ A Dm

in the love that on - ly you can give.
comes to peace in you, who makes us
know - ing that you al - ways make things new.
your love has the pow'r life to sus -
till the bit - ter end of ev - ery "Why."
through the cross we nev - er live in

F C Dm B♭ A

whole.
tain.
vain.

Refrain

Al-ways I am near you, God of rest and peace, all my long-ing for your care you know.

in your love a - lone my love may grow.

117 Tik brīniški, mans Dievs

How wonderful, my God

E. Wankin, Latvia

A. Krauklis, Latvia

Latvian:
1. Tik brī - niš - ki, mans Dievs, Tu ma - ni va - di. Dus Ta - vās ro - kās ma - ni dzī - ves ga - di. Kad nos - kumst sirds, Tu ma - ni mie - ri - ni. Tik brī - niš - ki.

2. Tik brī - niš - ki, mans Dievs, Tu ma - ni va - di. Kad sa - tumst nakts, man zvaig - žnu gais - mu rā - di. Kad kā - ja slīd, man ro - ku sat - ve - ri, Tik brī - niš - ki.

3. Tik brī - niš - ki, mans Dievs, Tu ma - ni va - di. Kad gai - sīs do - mas, ap - tum - šo - sies ska - ti, Man ro - ku sniedz un mā - jās pār - ve - di, Tik brī - niš - ki.

How wonderful, my God 118
Tik brīniški, mans Dievs

E. Wankin, Latvia
Eng. trans., S T Kimbrough, Jr., USA

A. Krauklis, Latvia

♩ = 76

1. How won - der - ful, my God, is your di - rec - tion. In your own hands my life en - joys pro - tec - tion. When my heart breaks, you com - fort, give me strength. How won - der - ful!

2. How won - der - ful, my God, is your di - rec - tion. Though dark - est night o'er - whelm me with de - jec - tion, you set the stars in heav'n to be my guide. How won - der - ful!

3. How won - der - ful, my God, is your di - rec - tion. When my thoughts fade and I see no con - nec - tion, you take my hand and safe - ly lead me home. How won - der - ful!

Eng. trans. © 2004 General Board of Global Ministries, GBGMusik, 475 Riverside Dr., New York, NY 10115.
All rights reserved.

119 Manchmal kennen wir
Sometimes we can know

Kurt Marti, Arnim Juhre,
Switzerland and Germany

Felicitas Kukuck, Germany
arr., Klaus-Dieter Köhler

1. Manch - mal ken - nen wir Got - tes Wil - len,
2. Manch - mal seh - en wir Got - tes Zu - kunft,
3. Manch - mal spür - en wir Got - tes Lie - be,
4. Manch - mal wirk - en wir Got - tes Fried - en,

manch - mal ken - nen wir nichts. Er -
manch - mal seh - en wir nichts. Be -
manch - mal spür - en wir nichts. Be -
manch - mal wirk - en wir nichts. Er -

leuch - te uns, Herr, wenn die Fra - gen kom - men.
wah - re uns, Herr, wenn die Zwei - fel kom - men.
glei - te uns, Herr, wenn die Äng - ste kom - men.
wec - ke uns, Herr, dass dein Frie - de kommt.

Sometimes we can know 120
Manchmal kennen wir

Kurt Marti, Arnim Juhre,
Switzerland and Germany
Eng. trans., S T Kimbrough, Jr.

Felicitas Kukuck, Germany
arr., Klaus-Dieter Köhler

1. Some - times we can know what God's will is;
2. Some - times we can see toward the fu - ture;
3. Some - times we can feel love, di - vine love;
4. Some - times we can make peace, di - vine peace;

some - times we can - not know. En -
some - times we can - not see. Pre -
some - times we can - not feel. O
some - times we do not care. A -

light - en us, Lord, when the ques - tions come.
serve us, Lord, when dread - ful doubts a - rise.
stay with us when o - ver - come with fears.
wak - en us, Lord, that your peace may come.

121 Savior of the nations, come

Martin Luther, Germany
Eng. trans., William Reynolds

Mary K. Jackson, USA

1. Savior of the nations, come;
Virgin's Son, here make your home! Marvel now, O
heaven and earth, that the Lord chose such a birth.

2. Not by hu-man flesh and blood; by the Spir-it of our God was the Word of God made flesh, wom-an's off-spring, pure and fresh. Come, Sav-ior, come.

122 Wonani kupswalwa ka Jesu
How wondrous the birth of Jesus

words and music, Zacharias M. Uqueio, Mozambique

Xitswa:
1. Wo - na - ni kup - swal - wa ka Je - su, ku - hla - ma li si le hi - nta - mo; wo - na - ni kup - swal - wa ka Je - su;
2. Va - ri - si va zwi - le a ge - zu, ti - thla - rit ti wo - no nye - le - ti; zi - va bye - la a ku me - si - a;
3. He - ro - di lo - ko a - zi - zwi - le, a - ku ho - si yi - be - lek - il - we; i lo xa ni se - kah hi - nta - mo,
4. Ha - zi - wo - na ho - si ya - hi - na, yi - ti - le ka - si ku po - ni - sa; ni - wi - hi lo y'a vu - me - la - ko,

123 How wondrous the birth of Jesus
Wonani kupswalwa ka Jesu

words and music, Zacharias M. Uqueio, Mozambique
Eng. para., S T Kimbrough, Jr.

♩ = 110

1. How won - drous the birth of Je - sus Christ!
2. The shep - herds heard an - gels sing on high;
3. When He - rod saw wise men from the East
4. We know Je - sus is Mes - si - ah come!

It filled peo - ple all a round with awe.
the wise men saw hea - ven's shin - ing star.
had come search - ing for the new - born child,
He's come sav - ing all the world from sin,

How won - drous the birth of Je - sus Christ,
All this showed that the Mes - si - ah's come
He said, "O I want to wor - ship him.
and those, who put all their trust in him,

for e - ven King He - rod was in awe.
with sal - va - tion for all hu - man - kind!
Tell me where to go to find this child?"
will find that by him they shall be saved.

1.

2.

Refrain

was in awe. Sing, hal - le - lu - jah! Sing,
hu - man - kind!
find this child?"
shall be saved.

ha - le - lu - jah! Sing, ha - le - lu - jah! to the Lord.

124 I have heard of a tree
(Heaven's Christmas Tree)

words and music, Charles A. Tindley, USA   arr. Charles A. Tindley, Jr.

1. I have heard of a tree, a great Christ-mas tree, it was fixed in yon Beth-le-hem's, Beth-le-hem's stall. The bless-ings of heav-en for you and for me, a

2. There is one I be-hold in let-ters of gold, it hangs on a limb near to, limb near to me. 'Tis la-beled "sal-va-tion," and Je-sus, I'm told, has

3. There is one just a-bove, it's ti-tle is love, it is marked by a deep crim-son, deep crim-son stain. For there it was tied by the Lord when he died, and

4. An-oth-er I see, it must be for me, the words "I will help you" I, help you I read. While hold-ing his hand, by faith I can stand, and

5. There are man-y, I'm sure, but just this one more I speak of a-bove all the, 'bove all the rest. It spells "hap-py home" with God near the throne, a

Christ - mas pres - ent for all.
bought that pack - age for me.
glo - ry to his dear name.
this is the pack - age I need.
place where the wea - ry shall rest.

Refrain

There is a pack - age for me on that tree; a

pre - cious to - ken that some - one loves me. Oh

yes, I can see on Cal - va - ry's tree, that

there is a pack - age for me.

125 Tout le ciel s'emplit
All the sky is bright

Claude Rozier, France

trad. melody, France
harm., M. E. Rose

French:
1. Tout le ciel s'em - plit d'u - ne joie nou - vel - le:
2. Le Seig - neur par - rait, ver - be de lum - iè - re
3. A - vec les ber - gers, a - vec tous les sa - ges,
4. Gloire à Jé - sus - Christ, gloire au Fils du Pè - re!

on en - tend la nuit di - re la mer - veil - le.
l'u - ni - vers con - nait la bon - té du Pè - re.
c'est le monde en - tier qui vers lui s'en - ga - ge
Gloire à son Es - prit dont l'a - mour é - clai - re

Fê - te sans pa - reil - le: Le Sau - veur est
Dieu de no - tre ter - re vient tra - cer la
pour voir le vi - sa - ge de l'a - mour vi -
l'é - cla - tant my - stè - re qui rem - plit le

né; l'en - fant Dieu nous est don - né.
voie oú che - min - e - ront nos pas.
vant qui pour nous s'est fait en - fant.
ciel: Gloire à l'hom - me Dieu! No - ël!

All the sky is bright

126

Tout le ciel s'emplit

Claude Rozier, France
Eng. trans., Fred Pratt Green, alt.

trad. melody, France
harm., M. E. Rose

1. All the sky is bright, filled with joy, a new joy.
Wait - ing for the night, we will talk of won - ders.
Nev - er was a feast like this: Born is Je - sus
Christ, born the Child - God given to us!

2. Now our Lord ap - pears, he whose word en - light - ens,
all cre - a - tion hears of the Mak - er's good - ness.
God is God of this poor earth and has come to
show where our wan - dring steps should go.

3. Not a - lone they come, sim - ple shep - herds, wise men:
all the hu - man race wants to make him wel - come,
wants to look up - on the face of the Lord of
bliss, who be - comes a child for us.

4. Glo - ry be to Christ, glo - ry to the Ma - ker's son,
and the Ho - ly Ghost, he whose love en - light - ens!
Daz - zling is the mys - tery fill - ing all the
sky: to the Child - God, "Glo - ry," cry.

127 Alilo Ots da khutsa amtvesa
On this blessed, holy morn

as taught by Ansor Erqomatshvile, Georgia
folk group Rustavi
Eng. para., S T Kimbrough, Jr.

trad. carol, Georgia

El niño ha nacido
Underneath a lean-to
(La noche de los pobres)

128

words and music, José María Santini, Uruguay
Eng. trans., S T Kimbrough, Jr.

Spanish: 1. El ni - ño ha na - ci - do ba - jo la en - ra - ma - da,
2. El ni - ño se duer - me, la ma - dre lo be - sa,

English: 1. Un - der - neath a lean - to Ma - ry birthed the Christ - child
2. As the child was sleep - ing, Ma - ry bowed to kiss him,

tie - ne la mi - ra - da a - zul.
le da su ti - bie - za un buey.
in whose eyes the world sees hope.
and the ox - en's warmth he felt.

Los sau - ces le me - cen can - cio - nes de cu - na,
Tra - en los pas - tor - es su a - mor de co - lor - es
And a lul - la - by came waft - ing from the wil - lows,
Soon ar - rived the shep - herds add - ing lo - cal co - lor,

Eng. trans. © 2004 General Board of Global Ministries, GBGMusik, 475 Riverside Dr., New York, NY 10115.
All rights reserved.

129

Esho hae Probhu
Come, O Jesus Christ

words and music, Bart Shaha, Bangladesh
Eng. trans., unknown

Bengali: E - sho hae Pro - bhu Tu - mi dho - ra yee - sho,
English: Come, O Je - sus Christ, make your dwell - ing with us.

Am - ra ro - ey - chi ja - gro - to.
We shall be watch - ful through the night;

Bho - rer - a shaye mo - ra ja - gro - to,
we'll wait with hope for your Day to dawn.

Muk - ti - da - ta tu - mi dho - ra yee - sho.
Come, set us free, all our trust is in you;

E - sho hae Pro - bhu Tu - mi dho - ra yee - sho.
now, O Je - sus Christ, make your dwell - ing with us.

Kindle a flame

130

words and music, John L. Bell, Graham Maule, Scotland

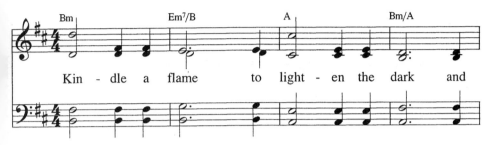

Kin - dle a flame to light - en the dark and

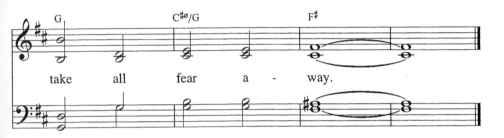

take all fear a - way.

See how great a flame expires,
kindled by a spark of grace.
Jesus' love the nations fires,
sets the kingdoms on a blaze.

To bring fire on earth he came,
kindled in some hearts it is;
O that all might catch the flame,
all partake the glorious bliss!

Charles Wesley

131 Ālōkaya āvā
God's own light came to earth

words and music, E. Walter Marasinghe, Sri Lanka

♩ = 92 Leader

Sinhala: Ā - lō - ka - ya ā - vā, ā - lō - ka - ya ā-

English: God's own light came to earth, God's own light came to

va, ā - lō - ka - ya ā - vā.

earth, God's own light came to earth.

Refrain (All)

No - sä - le - na no - mä - le - na ki - si di - na

Such a light as nev - er fal - ters, light of hope that

no - ni - ve - na, ā - lō - ka - ya ā - vā sa

nev - er al - ters, God's own light came to earth for

(to CODA) ⊕

dā - ta - na, ā - lō - ka - ya ā - vā.

all peo - ple, God's own light came to earth.

Leader

1. I - tā du - rin ä - ti yu - dā de - sē si - ta
2. Gä - li pa - vē duk vin - di - na an - an - ta - vu

1. Day - break in Ju - dah, the birth - day of Je - sus,
2. As night sur - ren - dered its phan - toms of dark - ness,

vi - da ka - lum da - sa di - gan ta he - li ko - ta
gi - li - si - ti - na mä -da a - vi -du an du ru mu -lu
sun - beams ap - pear, the ho - ri - zon is fill - ing up with
sun - shine be - gan to a - wak- en the hap - pi - ness of

sa - dä ta - ni - ka - le - sa e - ka - lu ka ra - na lo - va:
le - vi da - nan ma - na nu - van a ya - lu:
sun - light to warm ev - ery cor - ner of the u - ni - verse
mil - lions of peo - ple a - ban - doned in - to slav - er - y:

All

ā - lō - ka - ya ā - vā, ā - lō - ka - ya ā-
God's own light came to earth, God's own light came to

D. S. ⊕ CODA Fine

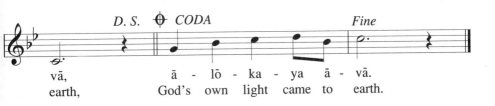

vā, ā - lō - ka - ya ā - vā.
earth, God's own light came to earth.

3. Dugi evan gava halen nagi ena
   maha paha neka sirin pura lana
   udamkarana nana vesin siyal dana
   alōkāya āvā.

3. New life has come from a stable so humble,
   rising to shine our own cities
   and countryside with beauty and joy
   to the end of all the centuries:

132 How deep our Maker's grief

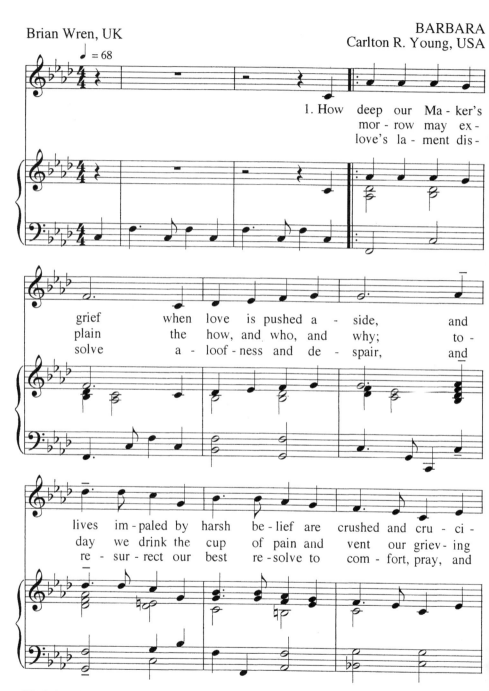

fied.
cry.
2. To- care.
3. Let

The text was first written in April 1993, after the death of children, women, and men in the Branch Davidian compound at Waco, Texas. It was revised, and shortened, in response to the bombings of the World Trade Center, New York City, and the Pentagon, in Washington DC, on September 11th 2001. This version, with this tune, was first sung at Cannon Chapel, Candler School of Theology, Emory University, Atlanta, GA, September 20, 2001.

Lord, make me an instrument of your peace;
where there is hatred, let me sow love;
where there is injury, pardon;
where there is doubt, faith;
where there is despair, hope;
where there is darkness, light;
where there is sadness, joy.

O Divine Master,
grant that I may not so much seek
to be consoled as to console;
to be understood, as to understand;
to be loved, as to love;
for it is in giving that we receive,
it is in pardoning that we are pardoned,
it is in dying that we are born to eternal life.

Francis of Assisi

133 Vos sos el destazado
You were tortured

words and music, Guillermo Cuéllar, El Salvador
from the *Misa Popular Salvadoreña*

Spanish: 1.-3. Vos sos el des - ta - za - do en la cruz,

1. que has ven - ci - do la mal - dad del mun - do, de - nun-
2. ma - sa - cra - do por los po - de - ro - sos; hoy de-
3. que con - stru - yes la paz con jus - ti - cia; a - yú-

cian - do al in - jus - to o - pre - sor, le - van - tan - do del
rra - mas tu san - gre tam - bién en la san - gre de
da - nos a no des - ma - yar, a lu - char por que

pol - vo a los po - bres. Te pe - di - nos que nos
nues - tros ca - í - dos. *Que tu paz lle - gue a no-
ven - ga tu Rei - no.

oi - gas, que es - cu - ches el cla - mor de tu pue - blo,
so - tros cuan - do ha - ga - mos bro - tar la jus - ti - cia.

te pe - di - mos que nos oi - gas,
Que tu paz lle - gue a no - so - tros

que es - cu - chés el cla - mor de tu pue - blo.
cuan - do ha - ga - mos bro - tar la jus - ti - cia.

Estribillo

Em B7 Am Em

* *last time only*

You were tortured

Vos sos el destazado

134

words and music, Guillermo Cuéllar, El Salvador
from the *Misa Popular Salvadoreña*
Eng. trans., Bret Hesla and Bill Dexheimer Pharris

1. You were tor-tured and nailed to the cross, but you've con-quered the forc-es of e-vil. You de-nounce the op-pres-sor a-bove, and you lift up the poor from the gut-ter. Now we beg you, hear, O hear us. Lis-ten now to the cry of your peo-ple. Now we beg you, hear us, hear us. Lis-ten now to the cry of your peo-ple.

2. You were tor-tured and nailed to the cross, you were slaugh-tered by pow-er-ful peo-ple. Now your blood, it is flow-ing a-gain in the blood of our mas-sa-cred mar-tyrs. *Let your peace now come a-mong us, when we act as a peo-ple of jus-tice. Let your peace now come a-mong us, when we act as a peo-ple of jus-tice.

3. You were tor-tured and nailed to the cross, but you're bring-ing us jus-tice and free-dom. If we stum-ble, O help us to stand and con-tin-ue to count-er op-pres-sion.

Refrain

* last time only

135 In our distress

S T Kimbrough, Jr., USA

Mary K. Jackson, USA

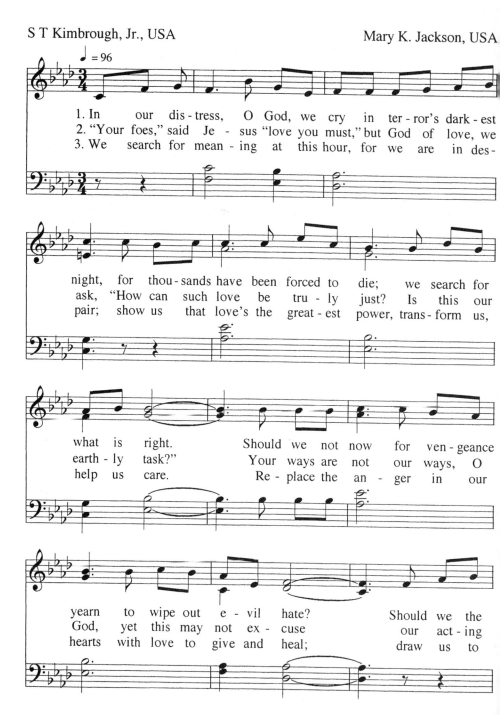

1. In our dis-tress, O God, we cry in ter-ror's dark-est night, for thou-sands have been forced to die; we search for what is right. Should we not now for ven-geance yearn to wipe out e-vil hate? Should we the

2. "Your foes," said Je-sus "love you must," but God of love, we ask, "How can such love be tru-ly just? Is this our earth-ly task?" Your ways are not our ways, O God, yet this may not ex-cuse our act-ing

3. We search for mean-ing at this hour, for we are in des-pair; show us that love's the great-est power, trans-form us, help us care. Re-place the an-ger in our hearts with love to give and heal; draw us to

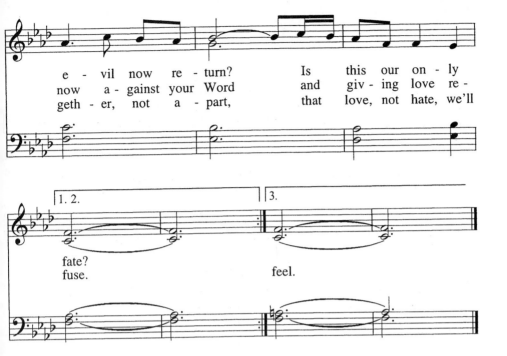

e - vil now re - turn? Is this our on - ly
now a - gainst your Word and giv - ing love re -
geth - er, not a - part, that love, not hate, we'll

1. 2.
fate?
fuse.

3.
feel.

The above text was written in response to the tragedy of the destruction of the World Trade Center towers in New York City and the damage to the Pentagon in Washington, DC on September 11, 2001.

Our earth we now lament to see
    with floods of wickedness o'erflowed,
with violence, wrong, and cruelty,
    one wide-extended field of blood,
where human fiends each other tear
in all the hellish rage of war.

O might the universal Friend
    this havoc of his creatures see!
Bid our unnatural discord end,
    declare us reconciled in thee!
Write kindness on our inward parts
and chase the murderer from our hearts!

Who now against each other rise,
    the nations of the earth constrain
to follow after peace, and prize
    the blessings of your glorious reign,
the joys of unity to prove,
the paradise of perfect love!

Charles Wesley

136 Přemohl Ježiž smrti noc
From death and darkness of the night

words and music, Luděk Rejchrt, Czech Republic

Czech:
1. Pře - mo - hl Je - žiž smr - ti noc. z hro-bu vstal na ú - svi - tu. Je - ho je slá - va, čest i moc a on nám krá - či na po - moc, na po-moc své - mu li - du.

2. To ji - tro ve - li - ko - noč - ní smiš chvá-lit v kaž - dém mís - tě. Vždyt' všu - de, kde, se shro - máž - dí ve jmé - nu je - ho dva neb tři, je s ná - mi zce - la, jis - tě.

3. Tak s cir - kvi svou se set - ká - vá ve svá - tos - tech a Slo - vu. Kaž - dé - mu, kdo jej poz - ná - vá, v po - kor - né vi - ře vyz - ná - vá, svůj ži - vot dá - vá zno - vu.

4. Je - ží - ši věr - ný, zů - statn již i s ná - mí, když den has - ne. At' nad hro - by, jež všu - de zřiš, nám sví - tí, ve - de dál a výš tvé, Pa - ne, svět - lo jas - né!

From death and darkness 137

Přemohl Ježiž smrti noc

words and music, Luděk Rejchrt, Czech Republic
Eng. trans., Jeffrey T. Myers, alt.

1. From death and dark - ness of the night,
2. His res - ur - rec - tion power ex - tends
3. In word and sign he comes, a - new
4. O faith - ful Je - sus, stay with us,

Christ rose as dawn was break - ing. He is the
through - out all times and plac - es. Where two or
a - gain his church cre - at - ing. To all who
when our last day is call - ing. Be al - so

glo - ry, power, and help now pour - ing forth as
three in Je - sus' name are gath - ering free, con -
speak his name and stand stead - fast to take their
there where our graves stand, and let the light that

new - born hope to all who are be - liev - ing.
fess - ing him, his Spir - it is de - scend - ing.
place by him, his love re - mains un - shak - en.
shone in you, on our way now be fall - ing.

138 Le tue mani son piene di fiori
You come with your hands filled

words and music, Marcello Giombini, Italy

1. Le tue ma - ni son pie - ne di fio - ri; do - ve li por-
2. I tuoi oc - chi ri - flet - to - no gio - ia; dim - mi, co - sa hai
3. Hai por - ta - to u - na ma - no al l'o - rec - chio; dim - mi, co - sa a-
4. Stai can - tan - do un' al - le - gra can - zo - ne; dim - mi, per - ché

ta - vi fra - tel - lo   mio?   Li por - ta - vo al - la tom - ba di
vi - sto fra - tel - lo   mio?   Ho ve - du - to mo - ri - re la
scol - ti fra - tel - lo   mio?   Sen - to squil - li di trom - be lon
can - ti fra - tel - lo   mio?   Per - ché so che la vi - ta non

Cri - sto ma l'ho tro - va - ta vuo - ta, fra - tel - lo mio!
mor - te,   ec - co co - sa ho vi - sto, fra - tel - lo mio!
ta - ne!   Sen - to co - ri d'an - ge - li, fra - tel - lo mio!
muo - re!   Ec - co per - ché can - to, fra - tel - lo mio!

*The "alleluias" may be sung in unison or in two parts.

139 You come with your hands filled

Le tue mani son piene di fiore

words and music, Marcello Giombini, Italy
Eng. trans., S T Kimbrough, Jr.

1. You come with your hands filled with flow-ers, and where did you
2. In your eyes I see joy o - ver-flow-ing. Tell me what you
3. With your hand at your ear did you lis - ten? Tell me what you
4. And I joined in the song of the an - gels. Tell me why you

take them, my dear friend? To the tomb of Christ Je - sus I
saw at the tomb, my friend. There I saw that death was de-
heard at the tomb, my friend. I heard sounds in the dis - tance of
sang at the tomb, my friend. O, I sang be-cause death is de-

took them, but found all was emp-ty at the tomb, my friend.
feat - ed, that is what I saw at the tomb, my friend.
trum -pets, and a choir of an - gels at the tomb, my friend.
feat - ed. That is why I sang at the tomb, my friend.

*The "alleluias" may be sung in unison or in two parts.

140

Yàlla mägg na
God indeed is great

Pentecost hymn, Senegal
Eng. para., S T Kimbrough, Jr.,
based on trans. by Nkemba Ndjungu

in the style of a call
to prayer from a mosque
transcr. by M. and C. Garrett

Wolof: Yàl - la mägg na, Yàl - la mägg na,
English: God in - deed is great, God in - deed is great,

Yàl - la mägg na, Yàl - la mägg na,
God in - deed is great, God in - deed is great,

Yàl - la ku sell - (e) Yàl - la ku sell la!
God is ho - ly, God is ho - ly!

A - ji mbë - geel - la, A - ji mbë - geel - la,
God in - deed is love, God in - deed is love,

A - ji mbë - geel - la. A - ji mbë - geel - la.
God in - deed is love, God in - deed is love.

Yàl - la du so - pi - ku, Yal - la du so - pi - u mukk!
God nev - er chang - es, God nev - er chang - es!

Ce'y Burr ta'l - la,   Ce'y Burr Yàl - la,
God rules our lives!   God rules our lives,

Yaay a - ji mägg ji, yaay a - ji mägg ji
God is the great - est, God is the great - est.

Sa xel mu ra - fet ni mu xoo - te.
God's Ho - ly Spir - it is glo - ri - ous,

Sa xel mu ra - fet ni mu xoo - te.
God's Ho - ly Spir - it is glo - ri - ous.

Yàl - la mägg na, Yàl - la mägg na,
God in - deed is great, God in - deed is great,

Yàl - la mägg na, Yàl - la mägg na,
God in - deed is great, God in - deed is great,

___ Yàl-la ku sell - (e) Yàl - la ku sell la!
— God is ho - ly, God is ho - ly!

* Leader sings notes with stems up, all sing notes with stems down. When singing the word "mägg," add a phonetic syllable "uh" on the second sixteenth note of the pattern. Pronunciation = "mägg(uh)".

141

Erwecke und belebe uns
Revive us and enliven us

Hartmut Handt, Germany

Horst Krüger, Germany

German: Er - wec - ke und be - le - be uns, du Geist der

Frei - heit. Er - leuch - te und be - we - ge uns, du

Hei - li - ger Geist.

1. Du schenkst die Frei - heit, Gott
2. Du gibst Ge - wiss - heit, dass
3. Du bist der Mut, der das

Va - ter zu nen - nen, machst uns zu Kin - dern im
Gott durch uns hand - elt, reisst uns aus Träg - heit und
Le - ben ver - wand - elt, machst Got - tes Bild in den

neu - en Bund. Du schenkst die
Angst her - aus. Du gibst Ge -
Glau - ben - den neu. Du bist der

Frei - heit, Gott Mu - ter zu nen - nen, du
wiss - heit, dass Gott durch uns hand - elt, du
Mut, der das Le - ben ver - wand - elt, in

D.C. al Fine

füllst mit Bit - te und Lob un - sern Mund.
stat - test mit dei - nem Ga - ben uns aus.
dir bleibt Gott dem Ge - schaf - fen - nen treu.

142 Revive us and enliven us
Erwecke und belebe uns

Hartmut Handt, Germany
trans., Philip R. Dietterich

Horst Krüger, German

♩ = 144-152   *Refrain*

Re - vive us, and en - liv - en us, you Spir - it of

free - dom. En - light - en and en - cour - age us, O

Ho - ly Ghost.   *Fine*
Spir - it of God

1. You give us free - dom to
2. You are the wit - ness that
3. You are the cour - age, the

Chord symbols: B♭ F/A Gm⁷ Dm/F E♭ E♭/F B♭ F B♭ F Gm¹ B♭/F E♭ F⁷ B♭ Gm Dm

143 Tout est fait pour la gloire de Dieu
All is done for the glory of God

words and music, Abel Nkuinji, Cameroon

French:
1. Tout est fait pour la gloi-re de Dieu, a - men! A - men!
2. La vie c'est pour la gloi-re de Dieu, a - men! A - men!
3. Le culte est pour la gloi-re de Dieu, a - men! A - men!
4. L'of - frande est pour la gloi-re de Dieu, a - men! A - men!

1.-4. Tout dé - pend de ce que tu en fais. A - men! A -

men! A - men! A - men! A - men!

Tout est fait pour la gloi - re de Dieu, a - men! A - men!

All is done for the glory 144
Tout est fait pour la gloire de Dieu

words and music, Abel Nkuinji, Cameroon
Eng. trans., S T Kimbrough, Jr.

1. All is done for the glo-ry of God. A - men! A - men!
2. Life is lived for the glo-ry of God. A - men! A - men!
3. We sing praise for the glo-ry of God. A - men! A - men!
4. All is giv'n for the glo-ry of God. A - men! A - men!

1.- 4. All de-pends up on our glo-rious God. A - men! A -

men! A - men! A - men! A - men!

All is done for the glo-ry of God. A - men! A - men!

145 And can it be that I should gain

Charles Wesley, Great Britain

Ludmila Garbuzova, Russia
arr., Carlton R. Young

1. And can it be that I should gain an in - terest
2. 'Tis mys - tery all: th' Im - mor - tal dies! Who can ex -
3. Long my im - pris - oned spir - it lay, fast bound in
4. No con - dem - na - tion now I dread; Je - sus, and

in the Sav - ior's blood? Died he for
plore his strange de - sign? In vain the
sin and na - ture's night; thine eye dif -
all in him, is mine; a - live in

me who caused his pain, for me who him to death pur-
first - born ser - aph tries to sound the depths of love di-
fused a quick - ening ray; I woke, the dun - geon flamed with
him, my liv - ing Head, and clothed in righ - teous - ness di-

146 Reamo leboga
We give our thanks to God

as taught by Daisy Nsakazongwe, Botswana
Eng., para., I-to Loh

transcr., I-to Loh

Tswana: Re - a - mo le - - bo - ga, re - a - mo le - bo - ga, re - a - mo le - bo - ga mo - di - mo wa ro - na.

English: We give our thanks to God, we give our thanks to God, we give our thanks to God, we give our thanks to God.

Often in African style of singing texts are improvised. The texts below are suggested improvisations by Andrew Donaldson.

We give our hands to you, (3x)
because you reached for us.

We give our eyes to you, (3x)
because you looked for us.

We give our feet to you, (3x)
because you walk with us.

We give our hearts to you, (3x)
because you first loved us.

Kiese! bu ngina mu Yisu 147
There's joy in living with Jesus

trad. words and music, Angola
Eng. trans., stz. 1, S T Kimbrough, Jr.
Helen Tobler-Staunton, stz. 2, alt.

Refrain

Kikongo: Kie - se! bu ngi - na mu Yi - su, bu ngi - na mu Yi - su, bu
English: There's joy in liv - ing with Je - sus, in liv - ing with Je - sus, in

ngi - na mu Yi - su. O - ma - yan - ngi! Mu ngi - la ya mo - yo
liv - ing with Je - sus! With my Je - sus be - side me there's light and

kie - na ye kon - so won - ga ko.
life and I'll nev - er be a - fraid.

1. Vo tu -
2. Vo lu -

1. When we
2. When we

vo - vi - lan - ga Yi - su mu mpo - vi - lu za kie - le - ka,
la nde ma Yi - su mu nda - ndu - lu lu ya kie - le - ka,

talk a - bout our Je - sus, and truth fills all we have to say,
fol - low Je - sus' foot - steps, and truth di - rects the path we take,

kie - na ye kon - so won - ga ko.
kie - na ye kon - so won - ga ko.

then we shall nev - er be a - fraid.
then we shall nev - er be a - fraid.

148 Somos pueblo que camina
We are people on a journey

from the *Misa Popular Nicaragüense*, Nicaragua

Spanish:
1. So - mos pue - blo que ca - mi - na por la sen-da del do - lor.
2. Los hu - mil - des y los po - bres in - vi - ta-dos son de Dios.
3. Es - te pan que Dios nos brin - da a - li - men-ta nues-tra u - nión.
4. Cris - to a - quí se ha - ce pre - sen - te; al reu - nir-nos en su a - mor.
5. Los se - dien - tos de jus - ti - cia bus-can su li - be - ra - ción.

Estribillo
A - cu - da-mos ju - bi - lo - sos a la san - ta co - mu - nión.

We are people on a journey **149**
Somos pueblo que camina

from the *Misa Popular Nicaragüense*, Nicaragua
Eng. trans., Carolyn Jennings

1. We are peo - ple on a jour - ney;
2. God has sent the in - vi - ta - tion
3. This is bread that God pro - vides us,
4. Christ is ev - er pres - ent with us
5. All who tru - ly thirst for jus - tice

pain is with us all the way.
to the hum - ble and the poor.
nour - ish - ing our u - ni - ty.
to u - nite us all in love.
seek their lib - er - a - tion here.

Refrain
Joy - ful - ly we come to-geth - er at the ho - ly feast of God.

150 Un mandamiento nuevo
Jesus a new commandment has given

John 13:34
English trans., Carolyn Jennings

William Loperena, O.P., Puerto Rico
arr., Luis Olivieri
and Roberto Milano

Spanish: Un man-da-mien-to nue-vo Je-sús nos dió.
English: Je-sus a new com-mand-ment has giv-en us:

que nos a-me-mos siem-pre co-mo nos a-ma
that we should love each oth-er just as our God loves

1. Dios.
us.

2. Dios.
us.

1. La se-ñal de cris-tian-dad
2. Quien al pró-ji-mo no a-ma,
1. The clear sign of all true Chris-tians
2. Those who do not love their neigh-bors

D   G   *D.C. al fine*

— es a - mar	se en her - man- dad._____
— mien - te si a_____	Dios di - ce que a - ma._____
— is the way_____	they love each oth - er._____
— do not tru -	ly love their Sav - ior._____

3.* Cris-to, Luz, Ver-dad y Vi-da
    al per-dón y a –mor in-vi-ta.

4. Per-do-ne-mos los a-gra-vios
    co-mo Dios ha or-de na-do.

5. De Je-sús her-ma-nos so-mos,
    si de ve-ras per-do-na-mos.

6. En la vi-da y en la muer-te
    Dios nos a-ma pa-ra siem-pre.

7. Don-de hay ca-ri-dad y a-mor
    siem-pre es-tá pre-sen-te Dios.

8. Co-mul-gue-mos con fre-cuen-cia
    pa-ra a-mar-nos a con-cien-cia.

9. Glo-ria a Dios el Cre-a-dor
    y a Cris-to el Sal-va-dor.

10. Y al Es-pí-ri-tu di-vi-no
    en Tri-ni-dad han vi-vi-do.

3.* Christ, the Light, the Truth, and true Life,
    bids us share our love and pardon.

4. Let us all forgive each other
    as by God we are commanded.

5. We are truly friends of Jesus,
    if we freely give our pardon.

6. In our living and our dying,
    God is ever there to love us.

7. In true charity and loving,
    God is ever there to love us.

8. Let us come to Jesus' table
    with our love for one another.

9. Glory be to the Creator;
    glory be to Christ, our Savior;

10. Glory be to God, the Spirit,
    Holy Trinity forever.

* A song for the passing of the peace; use stanzas as needed.

151 Pais ka lau pa ku
From this time onwards

Bunun hymn, Taiwan
transcr., I-to Loh, Taiwan

Bunun melody, Taiwan

Bunun:
1. Pais ka lau pa ku u* i hi, mal ma na nu u i hi.
2. Ta atha ha li nga u i hi, min sial is ang u i hi.
3. Ku da da tha, u i hi, mus kun Ta ma, u i hi.

Lis ka ta ma u i hi, ma dai dath tai - san u i hi.
Ta hus du ma u i hi, min a mu bu nun u i hi.
Ni tu ma tath, u i hi, na sa u haas, u i hi.

* Non-lexical syllables. These syllables sung by the Bunun tribal people are the equiv
of a congregational "Amen" in support of the leader.

From this time onwards 152
Pais ka lau pa ku

Bunun hymn, Taiwan
transcr., I-to Loh, Taiwan
Eng. para., James Minchin

Bunun melody, Taiwan

♩ = 80

Leader ... All ... Leader ... All

1. From this time on-wards, u* i hi, let's strive hard-er u i hi.
2. Hear God's word to us, u i hi, love each oth-er, u i hi,
3. God is call-ing us, u i hi, "Look to Je-sus, u i hi,

Leader ... All ... Leader ... All

trust-ing Je-sus, u i hi, be-ing neigh-bor-ly. u i hi.
walk to-geth-er; u i hi, live in har-mo-ny. u i hi.
death de-fy-ing, u i hi, he's vic-to-ri-ous!" u i hi.

* Non-lexical syllables. See note on previous page.

153 In mission together

words and music, S T Kimbrough, Jr., USA   refrain and arr., Jorge Lockward

1. We come from the moun - tains, the val - leys and plains, the cit - ies and farm - land a - wait - ing the rains. Our cul - tures are man - y, our tongues ev - en more; our
2. Though diff' - rent in cul - ture and modes of our dress, tho' strange seem our lan - guage we bold - ly con - fess that we are u - nit - ed: one peo - ple, one voice. We're
3. In Christ we're u - nit - ed, all bar - ri - ers fall; there's no fav - ored gen - der, one fam' - ly for all: op - pressed, rich, and need - y, the weak and the strong one

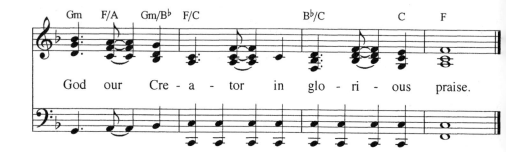

God our Cre-a-tor in glo-ri-ous praise.

154 Na nzela na lola
As long as we follow

words and music, Joseph Kabemba, Congo

Lingala:
1. Na nze-la na lo-la to-ko-tam-bo-la ma-lem-be, ma-lem-be to-ko-tam-bo-la.
2. Na nze-la na lo-la to-ko-yem-ba na e-se-ngo ma-lem-be to-ko-tam-bo-la.
3. Na nze-la na lo-la to-ko-te-ya na e-se-ngo ma-lem-be to-ko-tam-bo-la.
4. Na nze-la na lo-la to-ko-bon-de-la ma-si-ya ma-lem-be to-ko-tam-bo-la.

Refrain
Ma-lem-be, _____ ma-lem-be, ma-lem-be to-ko-tam-bo-la.

As long as we follow   **155**
Na nzela na lola

words and music, Joseph Kabemba, Congo
Eng. trans., S T Kimbrough, Jr., stz. 1, refrain
Carolyn Kappauf, stzs. 2-4, alt.

1. As long as we fol-low in the way that God is lead-ing, we
2. As long as we hope there is a fu-ture for cre-a-tion, a

know God's reign will sure-ly come. We know this_____ we
fu-ture for the u-ni-verse.

know this. Yes, God's reign will sure-ly come.

For stanzas 3 and 4 substitute the words "pray" (or "sing") and "act" for the word
"hope" in the first measure of stanza 2, and use the remainder of text of stanza 2 as is
for stanzas 3 and 4.

156   God's justice will come

words and music, Timothy E. Kimbrough, USA
para., Hos. 6:1-3

God's jus-tice will come like a shower, like rains that wa-ter the earth. God's jus-tice will come like a shower. O praise the name of the Lord.

1. Come, let us re-turn to our God who has struck us but binds up our
2. Let us strive to know the Lord, whose jus-tice dawns like the

Dm⁷   Am⁷   Gm⁷   Dm   G⁷/⁹

wounds.   Come, let us re-turn to our God.   O
sun.   Let us strive to know the Lord.   O

C⁷   A   Dm⁷   Am⁷   Dm   A♭º⁷

D.C. al Fine

praise   the name of the Lord.
praise   the name of the Lord.

Gm⁷   C⁷   F   Gm⁷/F   F   Gm⁷/F

157 Ayyuhal masslubu zulman
So much wrong

Jubrail Gabbour

Melody from Christian communities of
Lebanon, Jordan, Syria, Israel, Palestine

Arabic: (translit.)

1. Ay - yu - hal mass - lu - bu zul - man ya - mu -
2. Sha - ja - ru z - za - i - tu - ni yah - nu bak - i -
3. Ya ha - bi - bi ay - yu lah - nen min sha -

na qal - bil - ka - iib. Ka - bi - di - har - rah wa
an Rab - ba - l - Ga - lal. Wa ta - nu - hu - l - Qud - su
ja - l - qal - bi - l - ha - zin yam - na - hu - r - ru - ha 'a -

qual - bi 'a - li - qon fau - qas - sa - lib. Wa ha -
huz - nan wa - tu - lab - bi - ha - l - gi - bal.
za' - an wa yu - sal - li - l - mu' - min - in.

bi - bi wa ha - bi - bi - ay - yu ha - len an - ta fih, dzuq - ta

ka' - sal - mau - ti kai - ma yah - ya sha' - bon taf - ta - dih.

Words © 1995 Strube Verlag, Munich. Used by permission.

So much wrong

158

Ayyuhal masslubu zulman

Jubrail Gabbour
Eng. trans., Jeffrey T. Myers, alt.

Melody from Christian communities of
Lebanon, Jordan, Syria, Israel, Palestine

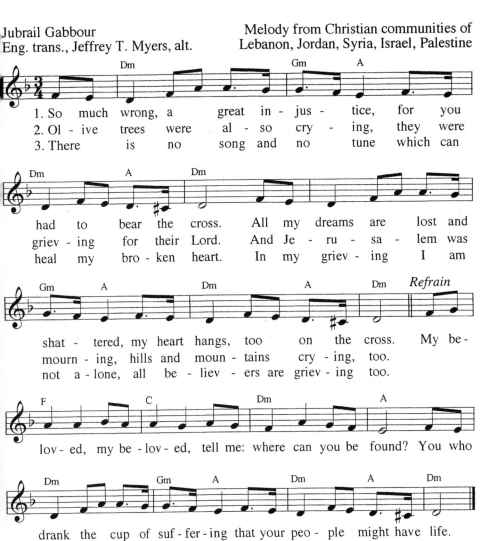

1. So much wrong, a great in - jus - tice, for you had to bear the cross. All my dreams are lost and shat - tered, my heart hangs, too on the cross. My be- lov - ed, my be - lov - ed, tell me: where can you be found? You who drank the cup of suf - fer - ing that your peo - ple might have life.

2. Ol - ive trees were al - so cry - ing, they were griev - ing for their Lord. And Je - ru - sa - lem was mourn - ing, hills and moun - tains cry - ing, too.

3. There is no song and no tune which can heal my bro - ken heart. In my griev - ing I am not a - lone, all be - liev - ers are griev - ing too.

159 Du satte dig selv
You came down to earth

Hans Anker Jørgensen, Denmark

Merete Wendler, Denmark

Danish:
1. Du sat - te dig selv i de ne - der-stes sted. Du sat - te dig oop mod de sto-res for - træd. Du sat-te dig ind i de y-der-stes nød. Du sat - te dig ud o - ver døds-angst og død.
2. Nu tal - er du til os fra hø - jes - tes sted, hvor ing-en kan ud - sæt - te dig for for - træd, og lev-er og lid - er dog med os end - nu, så ing - en er me - re i liv - e end du.
3. Du kæmp-er i ver-den for fri-hed og fred. Når an - dre gir op, blir du vil - je-fast ved. Du føl-ger os ind i den y-der-ste nød, og kal - der os ud af den in - der - ste død.
4. Du send-er os ned i de ned - er - ste sted. Du sæt-ter os op mod de stor-es for - træd. Du lev-er i os i de in-der-ste lag. Vi lev - er i dig på den y - der - ste dag.

A ma ta a-lu

We are one in Christ

160

as taught by Victor Avase, Uganda

Leader

A ma ta a - lu   A ma ta a - lu Je - su ma' al - ia.
We are one in Christ,   we are all u - nit - ed.   We are one in

All

A ma ta a - lu   A ma ta a - lu Je - su ma' al - ia.
Je - sus Christ our Lord.   We are one in Je - sus Christ our Lord.

161 You came down to earth
Du satte dig selv

Hans Anker Jørgensen, Denmark
Eng. trans., Per Harling, alt.

Merete Wendler, Denmark

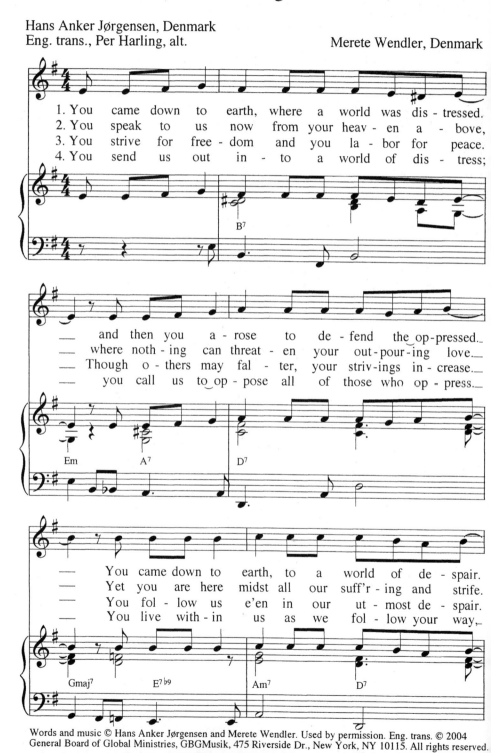

1. You came down to earth, where a world was dis-tressed,
2. You speak to us now from your heav-en a-bove,
3. You strive for free-dom and you la-bor for peace.
4. You send us out in-to a world of dis-tress;

— and then you a-rose to de-fend the op-pressed.
— where noth-ing can threat-en your out-pour-ing love.
— Though o-thers may fal-ter, your striv-ings in-crease.
— you call us to op-pose all of those who op-press.

— You came down to earth, to a world of de-spair.
— Yet you are here midst all our suff'r-ing and strife.
— You fol-low us e'en in our ut-most de-spair.
— You live with-in us as we fol-low your way,

You came down to earth, death and dy - ing to share.
You are the way; you are the truth and the life.
You bring us out from ev - ery in - ter - nal snare.
and we live in you on life's ve - ry last day.

Gmaj7   Em   C7   B7

1. 2. 3.   4.

Em   A   Em   Em   A   Em

162 Pelas dores deste mundo
For the troubles and the sufferings

words and music, Rodolfo Gaede Neto, Brazil
English trans, Simei Monteiro and Jorge Lockward

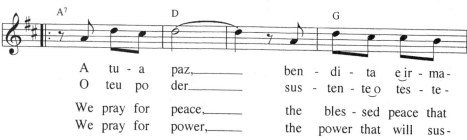

♩ = 80

Portuguese:
Pe - las do - res des - te mun - do, ó Se - nhor,___
Teus ou - vi - dos se in - cli - nem ao cla - mor___

English:
For the trou - bles and the suf - ferings of the world,___
Lend an ear to the ris - ing cry for help___

— im - plo - ra - mos pi - e - da - de.
— des - ta gen - te o - pri - mi - da.
— God, we call up - on your mer - cy:
— from op - pressed and hope - less peo - ple.

um só tem - po ge - me a cri - a - ção.
pres - sa - te com tu - a sal - va -
whole cre - a - tion's la - bor - ing in pain!
Has - ten your sal - va - tion, heal - ing

ção.
love!

A tu - a paz,___ ben - di - ta e ir - ma-
O teu po der___ sus - ten - te o tes - te-
We pray for peace,___ the bles - sed peace that
We pray for power,___ the power that will sus-

na - da co'a jus - ti - ça_____ a - bra - ce o mun - do in-
mu - nho do teu po - vo._____ Teu Rei - no ve - nha a
comes from mak - ing jus - tice,_____ to cov - er and em -
tain your peo - ple's wit - ness:_____ un - til your King - dom

tei - ro.   Tem com - pai - xão!

brace us.   Have mer - cy, Lord!

nos! Ky - ri - e e - le - i - son!

come, Ky - ri - e e - le - i - son!

Help us to proclaim 163

words and music, Simei Monteiro, Brazil

Help us to pro - claim   the year of grace, O Lord!

Help us to pro - claim   the

year of grace, O Lord!_____ Help us, Lord.

164 Prabhoo Lay lay mujhay
O Lord Jesus, enfold me

words and music, Samuel Paul, Pakistan

Urdu: 1. Pra - bhoo Lay lay muj - hay Too Ba - hoñ Meñ ka - heen
gir na ja - aun gu - naa hon meñ.
1. Me - ra tan man aur
2. Me - ray dil ko too
3. Paa - pe e - on ko

dhan te - ray lee - ay, me - ra sa - ra jee - van te ray lee -
ap - nay ruh say bhar; me - ray dil ho se - raf te - ra ni
main laau te - ray pass Ab - di ku - shi pa - en jo hain ud

1. Am ay. 1. Me - ra ay. | 2. Am E Am
ghar. 2. Me - ray ghar. Mu - jay lay chal tu ap nee ra - hon
aas. 3. Paa - pe aas. Too he too ho me - ree ni - gaa - hon
Vo bhee jaa - en te - ray ga - vaa - hon

D. C. al Fine

May, ka - heen gir na jaa un gu naa hon meñ. | 1. E Mu - jay meñ. | 2. E
may, ka - heen gir na jaa un gu naa hon meñ. Too he meñ.
may. Ka - heen gir na jaa un gu naa hon meñ. Vo bhee meñ.

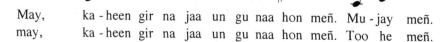

Words and music © 1995 Strube Verlag, Munich. Used by permission.

O Lord Jesus, enfold me 165
Prabhoo Lay lay mujhay

words and music, Samuel Paul, Pakistan
Eng. trans., Shirley Erena Murray, New Zealand

Refrain

O Lord Je - sus, en - fold me in your arms, let me

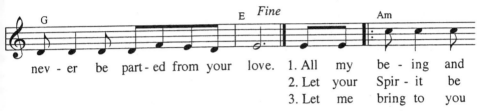

nev - er be part - ed from your love.
1. All my be - ing and
2. Let your Spir - it be
3. Let me bring to you

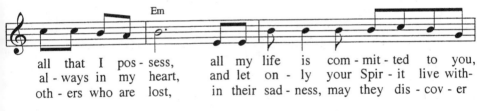

all that I pos - sess, all my life is com - mit - ted to you,
al - ways in my heart, and let on - ly your Spir - it live with -
oth - ers who are lost, in their sad - ness, may they dis - cov - er

Lord. All my Lord, come and turn all my foot - steps to your
in. Let your in, let my vi - sion be on - ly what you
joy. Let me joy, in be - liev - ing, they'll wit - ness to your

D.C. al Fine

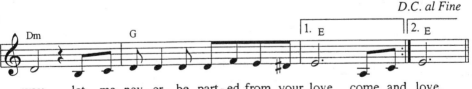

way, let me nev - er be part - ed from your love, come and love.
are, let me nev - er be part - ed from your love, let my love.
truth, let me nev - er be part - ed from your love, in be - love.

166

El amor
Only love

Words and music, Rafael Grullón, Dominican Republic
Adapt. from 1 Cor. 13
Eng. trans., S T Kimbrough, Jr.

harm., Jorge Lockward

Spanish:
1. El a -mor, el a -mor es su- fri - do y sa - cri - fi - cial. Quien a - ma es ca - paz de mo - rir; quien
2. El a -mor, el a -mor nun - ca pien - sa só - lo pa - ra sí; se go - za siem - pre de la ver - dad, per -

English:
1. On -ly love, on - ly love suf -fers all and sa - cri - fi -ces all. It dares to risk and face e - ven death; it
2. On -ly love, on - ly love thinks of o - thers, not just of it - self, re - joi - ces not in wrong but in truth; for -

167 Tu fidelidad
I depend upon your faithfulness

words and music, Miguel Cassina, Mexico
Eng. words, Andrew Donaldson

arr., Andrew Donaldson

Spanish: Tu fi - de - li - dad es grand - de.
English: I de - pend up - on your faith - ful - ness.

Tu fi - de - li - dad in - com - pa - ra - ble es.
I can jour - ney on for you are al - ways there.

Na - die co - mo tú, ben - di - to Dios,
None com - pare with you, O bless - ed One;

gran - de es tu fi - de - li - dad.
great is your faith - ful - ness.

Don'na tokidemo
Anytime and anywhere

unko Takahashi, Japan
ng. trans., James Brumm and Emily Brink

Schin'ichi Takanami, Japan

♩ = 100

Japanese:
1. Don - 'na to-ki-de-mo, don - 'na to-ki-de-
2. Don - 'na to-ki-de-mo, don - 'na to-ki-de-
(translit.)

English:
1. An - y - time and an - y - where know that Je - sus' love is
2. An - y - time and an - y - where know that Je - sus' love is

mo ku-ru-shi-mi-ni ma-ke-zu, ku-ji-
mo shi-a-wa-se-o no-zo-mi, ku-ji-
there. When in grief and loss, when in pain, God will
there. Don't des-pair, for God is kind. Look for

ke - te-wa na-ra-na - i. Ie-su sa-ma-no, Ie - su
ke - te-wa na-ra-na - i. Ie-su sa-ma-no, Ie - su
strength-en and sus - tain. Put your hope in God; trust God's
joy and you will find. Put a-way your fear; God is

sa - ma - no a - i o shi-n-ji - te.
sa - ma - no a - i ga a-ru-ka-ra.
ho - ly Word ev - ery time and ev - ery - where.
ver - y near ev - ery time and ev - ery - where.

Words and music © 2000 United Church of Christ in Japan. Used by permission. Eng. trans. © 2001 CRC Publications. Used by permission.

169

Ghuri ulach
My God, I love you

Traditional hymn, Algeria
Eng. para., S T Kimbrough, Jr.
based on a trans. by Guernine Hamid

♩ = 132
Refrain

Berber: (translit.) Ghu - ri u - lach, win a - zi - zen am ketch,
English: My God, I love you more than all;

Ghu - ri u - lach, win egh - la - yen am ketch,
noth - ing can be more wor - thy than you.

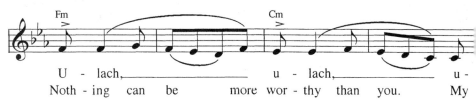

U - lach, u - lach, u -
Noth - ing can be more wor - thy than you. My

lach, win a - zi - sen am ketch U - lach,
God, I love you more than all. Noth - ing can

be more wor - thy than you. My God, I
u - lach, u - lach, win

Berber translit. and Eng. para. © 2004 General Board of Global Ministries, GBGMusik, 475 Riverside Dr., New York, NY 10115.

egh - la - yen am ketch._____
love you more than all._____

1. Ghu - ri egh - la -
2. Ah - nin e ssou
1. Wor - thy are you,
2. When I hear your

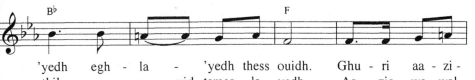

'yedh egh - la - 'yedh thess ouidh. Ghu - ri aa - zi -
thik ma - ra yid tsmes - la - yedh. Aa - zis wa wal
God, how I de - pend on you. You're the ve - ry
voice, it's sweet - ness to my ears. No word can com-

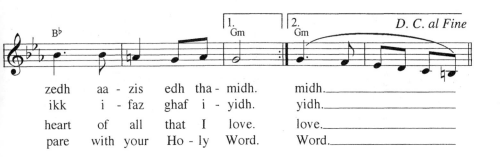

zedh aa - zis edh tha - midh. midh._____
ikk i - faz ghaf i - yidh. yidh._____
heart of all that I love. love._____
pare with your Ho - ly Word. Word._____

170 Vær sterk, min sjel
Be strong, my soul

Svein Ellingsen, Norway

Egil Hovland, Norway

Norwe-
gian:
1. Vær sterk, min sjel, i den - ne tid, når du har tungt å
2. Gi hå - pet rom i den - ne tid, hvor langt du enn er
3. Se, mør - ket blir din mod - nings - tid! Hold ut til nat - ten

bæ - re. Hold ut i prø - vens stund og lid de døgn du
ne - de. Hos dem som tap - er i sin strid, er Her - ren
ven - der! Se bort fra angst og in - dre splid, du er i

går i læ - re. En dag til slutt blir
skjult til ste - de. Ved Kris - ti verk skal
go - de hen - der! Se, du er fri og

mør - ket brutt av ly - set fra Guds frem - tid.
du bli sterk og hvi - le i Guds frem - tid.
lev - er i Guds løft - es - ri - de frem - tid.

Be strong, my soul

171

Vær sterk, min sjel

Svein Ellingsen, Norway
Eng. trans., Gerald Thorson

Egil Hovland, Norway

1. Be strong my soul, from day to day; let not your
2. Leave room for hope from day to day, when grief of
3. Look, dark - ness strength - ens you to - day, the morn - ing

trials de - tain you. En - dure the fight run not a -
loss de - ludes you. Al though you weak - en on the
shall sur - round you! Be not a - fraid keep dread a -

way from strug - gles that sus - tain you. The day a -
way, the hid - den God in - cludes you. Through Christ's one
way, God's arms are now a - round you. Look, you are

wakes when dark - ness breaks washed by the light of God's day.
deed, you shall in - deed, en - joy your rest in God's day.
free, a - live to see, the prom - ise of God's day.

172 En medio de la guerra
Amid the pain of war

Mario Bustamante, Bolivia
arr., Jorge Lockward

E. Jones

Spanish: 1. En
2. En
3. En

me - dio de la gue - rra y la mi - se - ria ce - le - bra - mos
me - dio de la du - da y de la nie - bla, ce - le - bra - mos
me - dio de la muer - te y del o - dio ce - le - bra - mos

la pro - me - sa, ce - le - bra - mos la pro - me - sa
la pro - me - sa, ce - le - bra - mos la pro - me - sa
la pro - me - sa, ce - le - bra - mos la pro - me - sa

de a - bun - dan - cia y paz.   En me - dio de la o - pre-
de es - pe - ran - za y fe.   En me - dio de los mie - dos
de vi - da y a - mor.   En me - dio del pe - ca - do y

F#   Bm   Bm

sión im - pues - ta, ce - le - bra - mos la pro - me - sa,
y trai - cio - nes ce - le - bra - mos la pro - me - sa,
de la rui - na ce - le - bra - mos la pro - me - sa,

A   G   D

ce - le - bra - mos la pro - me - sa de la li - ber - tad.
ce - le - bra - mos la pro - me - sa de soli - da - ri - dad.
ce - le - bra - mos la pro - me - sa de la sal - va - ción.

G   D   F#   Bm

Estribillo

To - dos jun - tos ce - le - bra - mos la pro - me - sa

del Se - ñor, to - dos jun - tos cons - tru - i - mos

la li - be - ra - ción. En ción.

Amid the pain of war

En medio de la guerra

173

E. Jones
Eng. trans., S T Kimbrough, Jr.

Mario Bustamante, Bolivia
arr., Jorge Lockward

1. A-
2. A-
3. A-

1. mid the pain of war and mi-ser-y we ce-le-
2. mid blurred vi-sion's fog and doubt-ful-ness we ce-le-
3. mid the blight of death and ha-tred's lie we ce-le-

1. brate God's won-drous pro-mise, ce-le-brate God's pro-mise of a-
2. brate God's won-drous pro-mise, ce-le-brate God's pro-mise that we
3. brate God's won-drous pro-mise, ce-le-brate God's pro-mise that we

bun-dance and of peace. A - mid op-pres-sion's dread-ful
shall have life and love. A - mid the dread-ful ruin and
shall have hope and faith. A - mid be-tray-als, fears, and

ty - ran - ny we ce - le-brate God's won - drous pro-mise,
pain of sin we ce - le-brate God's won - drous pro-mise,
hate-ful lies we ce - le-brate God's won - drous pro-mise,

ce - le - brate the pro-mise that we shall be free in-deed.
ce - le - brate that God has prom-ised sav-ing grace to all.
ce - le - brate the prom-ise of our sol - i - dar - i - ty.

Refrain

Al - to - geth - er let us ce - le - brate the pro - mise

A   D   F#

of our God.   Al - to - geth - er let us build a

Bm   A   D

world of li - ber - ty   A - ty.

| 1. 2. | 3. |

F#   Bm   Bm

174

Novo é o caminho
Let us walk a new way

words and music, Sifredo Teixeira, Portugal
Eng. trans., S T Kimbrough, Jr.

Portuguese: No - vo é o ca - mi - nho a per - cor - rer.
English: Let us walk a new way; come now, let's go.

No - va é a vi - da que es - tá pa - ra a - con - te - cer, En-
Let us dream a vi - sion, for it sure - ly will be so. Then

tão bro - ta - rá a paz, a a - le - gri - a e o pra - zer,
peace, glad-ness, joy shall bloom till the earth their flow'rs re - ceive,

e se - re - mos to - dos um, no no - vo vi - ver.
till all peo - ple one shall be and new life learn to live.

A es - pe - ran - ça não se po - de es - va - ne - cer,__
Hope is e - ter - nal, no one can its power de - stroy.

é im - por - tan - te a ju - da, nos - so que - rer.
Hope is im - por - tant to our wills and breeds joy.

Yarabba ssalami
You, God of peace

175

author unknown

trad. Palestinian melody
arr. Arne Lundmark

176   Que no caiga la fe
Where there's faith, there is hope

words and music, Eseario Rodríguez, Venezuela
based on a song by Carlos Ruiz
Eng. trans., S T Kimbrough, Jr.

Estribillo/Refrain

Spanish: Que no cai - ga la fe, que no

English: Where there's faith, there is hope, there's a

cai - ga la es - pe - ran - za   Que no cai - ga la

rea - son to be liv - ing.   Keep the faith, live with

fe, mi her - ma - no, que no cai - ga la fe, mi her - ma - na.

hope, my bro - ther; keep the faith, live with hope, my sis - ter.

Que no cai - ga la fe, que no cai - ga la es - pe -

Where there's faith there is hope, there's a rea - son to be

Fine

ran - za   Si se ca - e la es - pe -

liv - ing.   When you think that there's no

ran - za   de   tu   pe - cho,   si se a -
rea - son   for be - liev - ing,   and your

ca - ba   el de - se - o   de lu - char,
strength to fight the fight is al - most gone,

no te ol - vi - des del ros - tro de tu pue - blo,
just re - mem - ber the fac - es of your peo - ple.

D.C. al Fine

y con - fí - a, que el Se - ñor te   sos - ten - drá.
On - ly trust God, who will be your strength and hope.

177 Nos volvemos a Dios
We return to our God

words and music, Gerardo Oberman, Argentina
Eng. trans., S T Kimbrough, Jr.

harm., Horacio Vivares

Hitotsuhu no
When a grain of wheat

Toyohiko Kagawa, Japan
Eng. trans., Frank Y. Ohtomo

Ushio Takahashi, Japan

Japanese: (translit.) Hi - to - tsu - hu no   mu - gi wa   o -
English: When a   grain   of   wheat,   in - to the   ground

- chi - ke - ri   chi - no   u - e
—— has   fall - en,   in - to the   cold

ni   ma - ta ha - e - i - zu - ru
ground,   and lies in   wait - ing for the   spring,

ha - ru   o   ma - chi - tsu - tsu
and   lies   in   wait - ing for the   spring;

ma - ta ha - e - i - zu - ru,   ha - ru o
this fall - en   grain   will rise to   life,   this fall - en

ma - - chi - tsu - tsu.
grain   will   rise to   life!

179 Some man dey ask me say
Someone may ask me why

as recorded by Frank Kamanda,
Charles Davies Memorial UMC,
Lumley Freetown, Sierra Leone

transcr. Kristin Markay
and Jorge Lockward

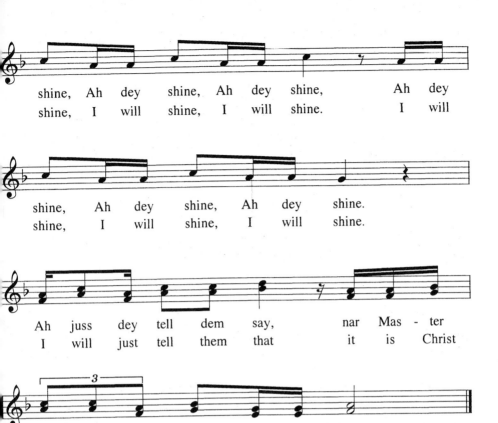

shine, Ah dey shine, Ah dey shine,   Ah dey
shine, I will shine, I will shine.   I will

shine, Ah dey shine, Ah dey shine.
shine, I will shine, I will shine.

Ah juss dey tell dem say,   nar Mas - ter
I will just tell them that   it is Christ

Ji - sus dey mek ah dey shine.
Je - sus that makes me to shine.

180 Ne pleure plus
Weep no more

words and music, Abraham Arpellet, Côte d'Ivoire
Eng. trans., S T Kimbrough, Jr.

French: Ne pleure plus, sèche tes larmes, lè-ve les yeux
English: Weep no more, dry your tears; to the hills of

vers les monts de l'es-pè-ran-ce.
hope raise your eyes and find new strength.

Mets en Jé-sus seul ta con-fian-ce,
When you put your trust in Christ a-lone,

a-lors ces-se-ra ta souf-fran-ce en-fin!
you will find that suf-fer-ing will cease at last!

Copyright Acknowledgments

Barry Chevannes
Dean's Office
Faculty of Social Services
Univ. of the West Indies
Mona, Kingston 7
Jamaica
barry.chevannes@uwimona.edu.jm

China Christian Council
169 Yuan Ming Yuan Road
3/F, Shanghei
200002 China
Tel. 011 86 21 6321 0806
Fax: 011 86 21 6323 2605
tspmccc@online.sh.cn

Choristers Guild
2834 W. Kingsley Road
Garland, TX 75041
Tel. 972-271-1521
Fax: 972-840-3113
choristers@choristersguild.org

Christian Conference of Asia
96, 2nd District, Pak Tin Village,
Mei Tin Road Shatin, New
Territory, Hong Kong
Tel. 852-269-1068
Fax: 2692-4378
cca@pacific.net.hk

david music
Riedtalstr. 14
4800 Zofingen
Switzerland
mail@davidpluess.ch

Andrew Donaldson
14 Hanley Ave.
Toronto, Ontario Canada
M4E 2R6
Tel. 416-691-1158
Fax: 416-690-9967

Éditions du SEUIL
Administered by SECLI
(see SECLI)

Estate of Frank Y. Ohtomo
c/o Mrs. Naoko Okumichi - Eisele
Koenigsteiner Str. 48
65812 Bad Soden /Ts.
Germany
Tel. & Fax: 06196-63611

European American Music
Distributors LLC
P.O. Box 4340
15800 NW 48th Avenue
Miami, FL 33014
Tel. 305-521-1794
Fax: 305-521-1638

Evangelical Lutheran Church in the
Republic of Namibia
P.O. Box 5069
Windhoek 9000, Namibia

Norbert Farrell
Parish of Barataria/Sixth Ave.
Malick, Barataria
Trinidad, The Caribbean

General Board of Global Ministries
GBGMusik
475 Riverside Drive, Room 350
New York, N.Y. 10115
Tel. 212-870-3783
Cscott@gbgm-umc.org

GIA Publications, Inc.
7404 S. Mason Ave.
Chicago, IL 60638
1-800-GIA-1358
timr@giamusic.com

Gustav Bosse Publishing House
Heinrich contactor avenue 35
34131 Kassel
Germany

Hinshaw Music Inc.
P.O. Box 470
Chapel Hill, N.C. 27514-0470
Tel. 919-933-1691
Fax: 919-967-3399
www.hinshawmusic.com

Hope Publishing Company
380 Main Place
Carol Stream, IL 60188
1-800-323-1049
Fax: 630-665-2552
hope@hopepublishing.com

Egil Hovland
Labräten 14 C
N-1614 Fredrikstad
Norway

Ivor H. Jones
1 Greenstone Terrace
Lincoln, England LN2 1PR
ivor.jones4@btinternet.com

Hans Anker Jørgensen
University of Copenhagen
Amager, Room 13.1.69
Njalsgade 80
DK-2300 Copenhagen S, Denmark

Arnim Juhre
Goerlitzer Str. 5
D-42277 Wuppertal
Germany

Kagawa Foundation
3-8-19 Kamikitazaw
Setagaya-ku, Tokyo, Japan

Les Éditions du Cerf
29 bd La Tour-Maubourg
75340 Paris Cedex 07, France

I-to Loh
117 Tungman Road, Sec. 1
Tainan, Taiwan
011 886 6 234 6060
Fax: 011 886 6 234 6060
lohito@ctinquiry.org

LTC
14-16, avenue de la République
94000 Créteil, France
Tel./Fax: 011 1 42 079263
www.ltc.asaph.com

Kurt Marti
Kuhnweg 2
Ch-3006 Bern, Switzerland

MCS America, Inc.
1625 Broadway, 4th Floor
Nashville, TN 37203
Tel. 615-250-4600
Fax: 615-250-4699

Mennonite Indian Leaders'
Council, Box 37
Busby, MT 59016

MOCISCALEB
Apartado 1025, Estado Lara
Barquisemeto, Venezuela

George A. Mxadana
Imilonji Kantu Choral Society
P.O. Box Orlando 1804
Soweto, South Africa

NEW-J Publishing
5312 North Capitol Street NW
Washington, D.C. 20011
www.nolanwilliams.com

OCP Publications
5536 NE Hassalo
Portland, OR 97213

Office for Worship
The Church of Scotland
121 George Street
Edinburgh, EH2 4YN
Scotland

Orden de Predicadores
Convento Nuestra Señora de
Rosario, Apartado 1968
Reparto Flamingo
Bayamón
Puerto Rico 00960-1968
Tel. 787-780-2613

Oxford University Press
198 Madison Ave.
New York, N.Y. 10016-4314
Tel. 212-726-6000

Pro Civitate Christiana
via Ancailani 3
06081 Assisi
Italy
Fax: 011 39 7581 3727
cep@cittadella.org

Dinah Reindorf
P.O. Box 13060
Accra, Ghana

José Antonio Ribas
Apdo 204, Zona 9-A
Panama

Heber Romero
Bellavista No. 28
El Ceiba Y Final Rpto. Escambray
Santa Clara C.P. 50200
Cuba

Samdan Publishers
P.O. Box 2119
Kathmandu, Nepal

Samen op weg wijkgemeente
Leeuwarden Camminghaburen
The Netherlands

SECLI
Abbaye Sainte Scholastique
F-81110 Dourne
France
Tel. 011 5 63 50 10 38
Fax:011 5 63 73 41 65
secli@secli.cef.fr

Singspiration Music (ASCAP)
Administered by Brentwood-
Benson Music Publishing, Inc.
(see Brentwood-Benson)

St. Mungo Music
Permissions
5 Beech Ave.
Glasgow G41 5BY
Scotland

Strube Verlag
Rights and Licencing
Pettenkoferstr. 24
80336 Munich
Germany
klaus.leitner@strube.de

Bart Shaha, Sec. Gen.
World Alliance of YMCAs
12 Clos Belmont
1208 Geneva, Switzerland
Fax: 011 41 22 849 51 10
secretarygeneral@ymca.int

The Copyright Company
1025 16th Ave. South, Ste. 204
Nashville, TN 37212
Tel. 1-800-779-1177
Fax: 615-321-1099

The Lutheran World Federation
150, Route de Ferney
P.O. Box 2100
Ch-1211 Geneva 2
Switzerland
Tel. 41 22 791 61 11
Fax: 41 22 791 66 30

The Pilgrim Press
700 Prospect Avenue
Fourth Floor
Cleveland, OH 44115
Tel. 216-736-3764
Fax: 216-736-2207
www.pilgrimpress.com.

United Church of Christ in Japan
2-3-18 Nishiwaseda
Shinjuku-ku
Tokyo 169-0051, Japan

Universal Edition
Administered by European
American Music
(see European American Music)

Verlag Singende Gemeinde
Westfalenweg 207
D-42111 Wuppertal, Germany
Tel. 001 49 202 7506 33
Fax: 001 49 202 75 53 04
info@cs-vsg.de

Walton Music Corp.
935 Broad Street #31
Bloomfield, N.J. 07003
Phone/Fax: 973-743-6444
www.waltonmusic.com

WGRG The Iona Community
Administered by GIA
(see GIA)

World Council of Churches
150, Route de Ferney
P.O. Box 2100
1211 Geneva 2, Switzerland
Tel. +41 22 791 61 11
Fax: (+41 22)791 03
www.wcc-coe.org

Yamuger
Jl. Wisma Jaya No. 11
Rawamangun
Jakarta Timur 13220
Indonesia
Tel. 062 21 475 81 48
yamuger@bit.net.id

Sir Colville N. Young
Office of the Governor-General
Belize House
P.O. Box 173
Belmopan, Belize

Zimbabwe East Annual Conference
c/o Patrick Matsikenyiri
No. 13 Cripps Road
Mutare, Zimbabwe
Pmatsike@su.edu

Zomba Songs Inc.
8750 Wilshire Blvd., 3rd Fl.
Beverly Hills, CA 90211
Tel. 310-358-4752

Index of Countries and Regions represented in *Global Praise 3*

*Great Britain, the name in use before the modern era, is used in reference to Isaac
 Watts, Charles Wesley, and John Wesley.

Index of Biblical References

Index of Composers, Authors, Translators, and Others

Index of First Lines and Common Titles*

*Common titles and first lines of texts without music appear in italics.